T0285231

100 YEARS

SIMON & SCHUSTER

DA BADDEST

KATRINA "TRINA" TAYLOR

with Sesali Bowen

Simon & Schuster

New York   London   Toronto   Sydney   New Delhi

100 YEARS

SIMON & SCHUSTER

1230 Avenue of the Americas
New York, NY 10020

First Simon & Schuster hardcover edition October 2024

SIMON & SCHUSTER and colophon are registered trademarks
of Simon & Schuster, LLC

Simon & Schuster: Celebrating 100 Years of Publishing in 2024

For information about special discounts for bulk purchases, please contact
Simon & Schuster Special Sales at 1-866-506-1949
or business@simonandschuster.com.

The Simon & Schuster Speakers Bureau can bring authors to your
live event. For more information or to book an event, contact the
Simon & Schuster Speakers Bureau at 1-866-248-3049 or visit our
website at www.simonspeakers.com.

Interior design by Joy O'Meara

Manufactured in the United States of America

1 3 5 7 9 10 8 6 4 2

Library of Congress Cataloging-in-Publication Data has been applied for.

ISBN 978-1-6680-0876-8
ISBN 978-1-6680-0881-2 (ebook)

To my niece Suga.
No matter where life takes me,
I will always find Sugaland.

Foreword

······· ◆ ·······

The first time I heard "Da Baddest Bitch," I remember thinking, *Who is this talking mad shit? She wildin'!* That was the first song I ever heard from Trina, and it wasn't like anything else that was out at the time. By then, Lil' Kim had opened the door for women to be risqué with their lyrics and even their style, but Trina was able to catch everyone's attention because she was bringing a completely different vibe being from Miami. *Play the player but don't ever get played!* Trina had this strong Southern accent, and her delivery was just hard. Even the beat for "Da Baddest Bitch" was different from anything else I had heard at that time. The song was just dope. Then when I heard the rest of her first album, I just knew: *This girl got some shit.*

I still remember the day we met. It was 2001, and I was getting my glam done at BET's Spring Bling when someone mentioned that Trina was there. I knew of her at that point, and I definitely wanted to meet her. As soon as she walked in, I could tell she was good people. Her energy was pure—that's the best way to describe it. We exchanged numbers, and I hit her up shortly after that, as I was working on "One Minute Man" and wanted her on the song. I knew she would go crazy on it! I sent her the song, but it took her some time to get to it. When she finally recorded her verse, she was hoarse and wanted to do it again, but to me, the raspiness actually made it better. And she of course went crazy on her verse—just like I knew she would. I told her, "This is IT right here!" With any track she jumps on, Trina always understands the assignment. She knows how to adapt to evolving sounds, generations, and trends without losing the core of who she is as an artist. That's why she's been able to transcend and stay relevant for so many years.

Trina's feature on "One Minute Man" was just the beginning for us. When we linked up to shoot the video, I knew I had made a dope friend for life. The whole time we were on set, we laughed and laughed like we had already known each other for years. It was one of those real connections from the start. In this industry, you run across a lot of people who end up being business associates, but finding a sisterhood is major, and Trina has been that—my sister—since we met over twenty years ago. I'll never forget the time I paid a spot to install some speakers in my truck and the employees had the nerve to joyride my whip around Miami! Trina went up to the shop and went off, on my behalf. She laid into them like it was her car. I could tell a dozen stories about the different times Trina has ridden for me like that. Trina is one of the most loyal people I've ever met and not just to me. There is nothing she wouldn't do for the people she really loves and cares about. She is the backbone for so many of her friends and family; she will stay ten toes down to make sure they're good.

What has always separated Trina from everybody else is that she's real. It comes across in her music, and it comes across when you're in her presence, even if you just met her. Her closest friends will tell you that she doesn't take bullshit from anybody, and she will put anyone in their place if need be. She's always good to have a laugh with and will crack a smile at the drop of a dime. But I've learned not to trust that smile all the time because she can go from zero to a thousand so quick. I'm talking seconds—hell, maybe half a second. Y'all have seen the "Light the blunt!" video. But all of that intense energy is there because Trina is real. She's a sensitive and extremely passionate person, and she's not the kind of woman who's going to pretend like she's not. But she's smart enough to use good judgment about which situations she puts herself in and who she can trust to be her full self around. When you know her story, you understand why. Her story is one of strength. You have to be strong to survive in this industry for as long as she has. People remember the raunchy lyrics and the sexy videos, but not a lot of people really understand the storms she's had to weather. I'm so proud of her for making it this far, and I'm glad that she's finally telling her story. Trina can teach anybody how to talk their shit and be a baddie living the good life, but the best thing you can learn from her about being the baddest is how to stay real and keep your head up through those dark times.

For almost twenty-five years, Trina has been a consistent presence in hip-hop. There is no denying that she has shaped the sound, the look, and the energy of today's female rap. Every time one of the mainstream female MC's songs or videos comes on, you can see and hear the blueprint that Trina laid out in 2000. What's so beautiful about her spirit is that she welcomes the new generation with open arms. Trina appreciates what they bring to the table because she knows what she brought to the table all those years ago. She celebrates the new girls, collaborates with them, and lets them learn from her wins and mistakes along the way. Trina is living proof that being a legend is not always about how many albums you've sold; it's about the *impact* you've had. I hope reading Trina's story will have a positive impact on your life, as I can tell you for sure—knowing Trina has definitely had one on mine.

—Missy Elliott

Chapter

1

My voice is such a distinctive part of who I am. It has a high pitch that can be raspy or sharp. It penetrates any track I'm on and makes my presence on a song that much more memorable. After the unapologetic, explicit lyrics, it's my voice that hooks people in my music. I didn't know just how far it would take me, but I was primed to use my voice from a young age. I was born into a huge family full of loud talkers, in a city that boomed with electricity and rhythm, in a neighborhood that was constantly radiating with energy.

My mom, Vernessa, was just a teenager when I was conceived unexpectedly, and it was anything but easy for her. It was the '70s, so she was forced to transfer to a high school for pregnant teens. Then, three weeks before I was born, she took a nasty fall that almost ended my unborn life and put her on bed rest until I was Earthside. But Vernessa was resilient. She hadn't planned on becoming a parent so soon, but she was determined to step up to the plate. Unfortunately, my biological father was not. Apparently he didn't want anything to do with fatherhood, and my mom was ready to raise me on her own. God had other plans. She met her husband, the man everyone called Mr. Wonderful, before I was old enough to remember. He raised me like I was his flesh and blood, and he was the only father I had. By the time I started kindergarten, we were a family of four that included me, my parents, and my sister, Laura, who is four years younger than me.

My immediate family was just the tip of the iceberg, though. Vernessa, who went by Nessa, was one of six siblings born to Bahamian parents in Miami. I had a whole network of aunts, uncles, and cousins who constantly shuffled between the city and the islands. On any given day, they would step in for my parents to get us to or from school, host sleepovers with our cousins, and celebrate our birthdays and holidays. My mom's youngest brother, Uncle Clifton, was regularly present in our lives before he passed away. He was a ball of energy and not as laid-back as her oldest brother, Vin. However, the women in my family were a different breed. My aunt Sheila was the professional businesswoman. She owned a bank and always looked so put together. Aunt Sany was never far away, with a joke to crack and a story to tell. A party was bound to happen when we had family in town from the Bahamas, but when my great-aunt Lou Lou came, Laura and I knew that we were losing the extra twenty minutes of sleep our mom normally let us have. She had traditional Caribbean values and didn't believe in young women participating in smacking their lips, putting their hands on their hips, leaving their bedroom without fixing their bed, or being late. She was loud about it, too. When she gave us marching orders to get out of bed, clean up, or get dressed, the whole house could hear it. We knew better than to challenge anything she said because it was customary to get your butt whooped for being disrespectful, but we couldn't wait until she went back home.

My parents lived in a four-bedroom house with a pool in Aventura, a suburb just north of Miami, but my grandmother's house in Liberty City was home base for my entire family. The modest single-story house with the short gate is where my grandparents raised my mother, her siblings, and their kids. It was there that I got used to the nonstop yelling, laughing, and singing. God forbid an argument break out. My family has always been animated and colorful. We love music, dancing, laughter, and joy. One of my uncles could tell a story, and listening to it was like watching a one-man show. Unlike a lot of moms who shushed the little girls they raised, Nessa pushed me to speak my mind because that was a sign of strong character and dignity. If she ever thought I wasn't saying something with enough confidence, she would say, "Girl, speak up!" I got comfortable expressing myself early because the people I respected the most encouraged me to do so.

In the summers, my skin was permanently tanned from playing up and down Sixty-Sixth Street in the blazing sun with other kids from the neighborhood—some of them my first, second, and third cousins. There were so many of us we could have started our own gang if we wanted to, but our only rival was our no-nonsense grandmother. She was a heavyset woman who never lost her smooth Bahamian accent. Unlike the rest of the family, my grandmother wasn't quick to raise her voice. We respected her words and rules so much that she only needed to tell us once to clean up or be quiet. If she got upset enough to yell, it was already too late. She ruled her house like a kingdom, perched near the open front door where she could catch a rare breeze and see what was happening inside and out at any given moment. My grandmother often spoke in parables. One time she told me, calm as day, "In *here*, there is nothing bigger than me."

That was the day my little-girl brain started to think my grandmother might actually be God. If not, she had to be the closest thing in human form. She commanded so much respect with just her presence, even from the adults in the family. Her power intimidated me sometimes because I didn't understand it, but I loved her.

My grandmother's house—the Taylor house—was a second home, and she was part of what made it comfortable. It was filled with the people I love and always smelled like a mixture of cleaning supplies and spices. My grandmother cooked island food on the regular. Boiled fish and grits. Johnnycake. Baked chicken. You name it, and she could whip it up in the kitchen. I come from a family of foodies, and my taste buds were developed on freshly cooked meals. There was never anything appetizing to me about fast food. Thankfully, everyone in the bloodline inherited my grandmother's cooking gene. We came together often for celebrations, for grief, for Sunday dinner, for huge weekend cookouts in Morningside Park, or sometimes for no reason at all. Whether it was a backyard bash at my mom's house or a cousin's sleepover at my aunt's, no one ever left hungry.

Laura and I both attended Liberty City Elementary School. It was only about a ten-minute walk from my grandmother's house. Nessa or Mr. Wonderful drove us to school from our house in Aventura in the mornings, and in the afternoons, we walked ourselves to our grandmother's. My cousin Stella, Aunt Sany's daughter, was closer to my age and made the after-school commute with me before Laura was old enough to join us. I knew the different routes like the back of my hand. We walked past some of the same faces every day, like the older woman who always sat outside of her duplex apartment and waved to us. Liberty City was my stomping ground, and I felt safe there.

One day when I was in fourth grade, Stella and I were on our normal route home. We were just two girls in a crowd of screaming kids excited to be out of school. I didn't have a care in the world except what we might eat and how much playtime we would have before my mom picked me up to head back to Aventura. Nothing was out of the ordinary until a loud screeching sound broke through the rest of the noise on the street.

The next thing I heard was Stella's screaming, and I realized I was on the ground. My face burned like someone had just touched it with a hot comb, and it was wet. A crowd of people gathered around me; some of them were trying to talk to me, but some of them were just hollering. Confusion took over my mind, but my whole body was in pain, especially my face. I started to panic, then I saw a pickup truck. It was so close—on the sidewalk with us where it didn't belong. Everything was just wrong. I wasn't supposed to be on the ground. Stella wasn't supposed to be screaming. My face and neck weren't supposed to be wet. I looked down, saw my bloody clothes, and wanted to scream or cry. Before I could do either, someone scooped me up into their arms, and I blacked out. It was the older lady from the duplex.

This time it was Nessa screaming. Only a few minutes had passed, and in that time the neighbor got Stella and I the rest of the way to the Taylor house. My mom was normally composed, even in a crisis, but the sight of her firstborn's bloody face made her hysterical. The force of her panic was enough to snap me back to consciousness. She put me in the car and sped me to the hospital. Thankfully, I looked to be in worse shape than I actually was.

We learned that the pickup truck spun out of control and jumped the curb, but by the grace of God, it didn't hit me. As it spun, a piece of wood hanging over the edge of its flatbed swiped me. It knocked me over and split my face open from my lip to my ear, but I didn't have any major nerve damage or life-threatening injuries. The wound was big, though, and I was at risk for an infection, so doctors still rushed me into surgery to stitch it up. They wanted to minimize the chance of me having a permanent scar, so the surgeon used a technique where the stitches were placed from inside instead of on top of my skin like they normally are. It turns out that Dr. Grossman, who did my procedure, was on the team of doctors who helped Richard Pryor recover from his burn injuries after he set himself on fire in 1980. Thanks to his blessed hands, my skin healed over the area naturally, and the only mark left from the accident is a small scar above my lip. I know my mom was so grateful that the lady from the duplex was compassionate enough to bring me home.

Liberty City had its problems, but there was a close-knit community there, and my parents were well-known in it. My dad owned a store on Sixty-Fourth Street, two blocks away from the Taylor house. Mr. Wonderful Grocery was the quintessential hood corner store in the '80s. The storefront was painted a dull blue with big black block letters. He had a pay phone attached to the wall outside and bars across the windows that had been painted to say MR. WONDERFUL GROCERY in fancy print. He sold candy, snacks, beer, grocery essentials, cigarettes, and cleaning supplies. Laura and I had free rein to explore and didn't have to pay for anything we wanted off the shelves. We knew exactly what the saying *kid in a candy store* meant.

The store was perfectly located in the middle of all the action in Liberty City. It was across the street from the Liberty Square projects—also known as the Pork 'n' Beans because the buildings were painted shades of burgundy and brown, the same colors you would find in a bowl of pork and beans—on the very busy Fifteenth Avenue. Local churches, restaurants, and houses lined the block, so there was constant foot traffic: kids running in and out for a sugar fix, men lingering around after they bought a beer or cigarettes to shit-talk, women pushing strollers back and forth, and people hopping out of cars with the music blasting. It seemed like all of them knew Mr. Wonderful, and he knew them. He couldn't make it from the curb to the door without someone greeting or stopping him to talk. Even the guys with thick gold chains and shiny rims on their cars, who made everyone stop and stare, would pull over, hop out, and shake my dad's hand. In the summers, he threw block parties outside the store that attracted the whole hood to come out. Sometimes he had speakers, a DJ, and huge smokers set up to grill hot dogs, ribs, chicken wings, and burgers. In the wintertime, he bought toys and handed them out of the trunk of his Cadillac. The neighborhood kids and their parents swarmed him, trying to get their hands on a little something extra to put under their Christmas trees. I loved knowing it was my dad bringing so much happiness to our community.

If Mr. Wonderful was the king of Liberty City, ruling from the throne of his corner store, Nessa was the gracious queen. She grew up on those same streets, so these were her childhood friends and neighbors. She was always warm and friendly with the people she interacted with, whether it was the local drunk or one of the church ladies. I could never tell a stranger from someone she'd known for years. In our family, she was the person people turned to for advice, support, or a little money if someone was in a tight spot. Sometimes she extended that same nurturing spirit to friends and people she knew from around the way. If she was hosting a party, everyone wanted to come. She was the woman you trusted to look out for your kids or help your elders.

Nessa was a beautiful person, inside and out. She hardly ever wore makeup, except for a little lip gloss, unless she was going out, but Nessa knew everything there was to know about beauty because it was her business. She was the go-to hairstylist in our family. She put ponytails in my and Laura's hair with precision, parting them different ways, adding bows and barrettes to match our outfits. She always made sure we felt beautiful. All the women in my family counted on Nessa to slick and mold their hair into updos and French rolls or give them a fresh silk press. She was a naturally gifted stylist (so is my sister, who still does my hair), but she was also licensed. When I was in middle school she opened her first hair salon, on Sixty-Fifth Street. She decorated it with pops of orange because that was her favorite color. Eventually, she rented out the attached space next door to the salon and opened her own beauty supply. She was one of the few Black women who sold weave, hair-care products, and styling tools because beauty supply stores were—and still are—mostly owned by Koreans. But it was such a smart business move because she could upsell the clients who came to get their hair done and turn customers who came in to buy products into clients.

.... ◆ ....

Even though my parents separated when I was in elementary school, I can honestly say my family gave me an amazing childhood. In my eyes, my parents were the epitome of cool and stylish. Mr. Wonderful was always in a new Cadillac, and Nessa had a walk-in closet full of clothes, purses, and shoes from designers like Louis Vuitton and Gucci. I didn't think we were millionaires, but Laura and I never wanted for anything. We could afford to eat at Red Lobster (back when it was considered a nice restaurant) if we felt like it, and we went on cruises to different islands. Sometimes Mr. Wonderful—who remained a constant presence in my life after he and my mom separated—would pick us up from school in a limousine just for fun. He knew I liked math, so his idea of a fun activity for me was to count out a trash bag full of cash to make sure I got the right number.

I walked around Liberty City with my head held high because I was the proud daughter of two of its most respected people. The only place I was wary of was the projects. The one rule that Nessa strictly enforced was that I should not, under any circumstances, be hanging out in the Beans. On Fifteenth Avenue, someone from her shop, my dad's store, or my grandmother's block could keep an eye on us. The projects were a huge maze of buildings that looked worse every year because the government, which built them, didn't bother to take care of them. Liberty Square was built in 1937 as the first public-housing project for Black people in the South. Whenever the city wanted to expand real estate development or build highways in other areas of Miami, they had to figure out where to ship the poor Black people who already lived there, and Liberty Square was the answer. For years, Liberty City was a middle-class neighborhood, where Black people like my grandparents owned most of the businesses and homes in the area. As the Beans filled with more people from different parts of the city who were struggling to get by, Liberty City started to decline. By the time I was born, the Beans had already seen its share of crime, shoot-outs, and race riots. But in the '80s, when Miami became the cocaine capital of the country, drugs took it to another level. Liberty City became one of Miami's roughest neighborhoods, and the Beans were at the center of it.

I met Pinkey on my first day at Charles Drew Middle School. We were in the same class and kept each other company all day to navigate our new environment. We did it again the next day and decided to walk home together. My middle school was even closer to the Taylor house than Liberty City Elementary—and just a block away from the Beans—but I was still happy to have someone to walk with. So was Pinkey. But we didn't get very far before she started to cross the street. I asked where she was going, and she said, "Home." She lived in Liberty Square. I wanted to keep hanging out, but as I looked at the drab buildings and all the guys standing around, I remembered Nessa's rule. "Come with me to my mom's shop," I suggested instead.

We became inseparable after that. The four years between Laura and me felt like a generation in middle school. Pinkey and I were the same age, and she became a second sister that

I could confide in about stuff like boys and periods. The problem was that we only got to see each other at school and for a few hours after when she could hang out with me at the shop or my grandmother's house. Like a lot of families in the projects, Pinkey's struggled to get by. All I had to do was ask my parents for what I needed, but it wasn't as easy for her to go to the movies, the mall, or out to eat. She was the person I wanted to hang out with the most, and for the first year, we navigated our different circumstances as best we could. Nessa did what she could to support my new friendship, letting Pinkey stay at our new house in central Miami for sleepovers. She often showed up at school with everything she'd need to stay overnight in her book bag.

With a new partner in crime by my side, I felt more confident to test my boundaries. Occasionally, I'd sneak into the Beans to hang out because I knew Pinkey would have my back if anything happened. There would be hell to pay if Nessa caught us doing anything we weren't supposed to, so we learned how to scheme and plan when we broke the rules. One day in eighth grade, we decided to play hooky from school. Stella, Pinkey, and I met in front of the school building and walked in the general direction of the door, pretending we were headed inside. When my mom was out of sight, we walked past the building and straight to my aunt Sheila's house. She worked at the bank during school hours, so I knew her crib was empty. The plan was to walk back to school in time to blend in with the crowd during dismissal. I thought our strategy was foolproof, and all of us were confident we would get away with it. We arrived at my aunt's and posted up outside to see what the day would bring, like it was a weekend. Within an hour, I recognized my mother's car speeding up the street. Our adventure was over just as fast as it had begun.

I had never missed school without Nessa's permission, so I didn't know they called the parents of children who were absent without an excuse. My mom immediately called around to other family members in the area asking if they knew my whereabouts. When none of them did, she started her own quick search of places she knew I was familiar with. Aunt Sheila's house was near the top of the list. Nessa glared at me as she threw the car in park and didn't say a word when she hopped out. She snatched me up by the collar of my shirt and dragged me to the passenger seat. Pinkey and Stella knew to get in the back seat behind us. My two accomplices and I remained quiet as Nessa verbally unleashed her fury in the car. The five-minute drive wasn't long enough for her to fully express that our plan was stupid and had caused her unnecessary stress and inconvenience. So she continued the tirade, loudly, as she escorted us into the school building, keeping a tight grip on my arm so everyone knew whose mother was causing a scene. The three of us were so embarrassed.

Nessa must have known I was the ringleader, because she still let Pinkey come around. If anything, we spent even more time together. Those weekday sleepovers turned into full weeks that Pinkey stayed at my house. I guess it was better for us to be close enough for my mom to keep an eye on us. I shared my clothes, hair products, and anything else I had with Pinkey without any hesitation, and I never judged her for her background. I was glad that she could enjoy the comforts of my house because I knew what life was like for some of the folks in the Beans. Our classmates in the projects were dealing with parents who were incarcerated, addicted to drugs, or dead. Some of them had eight or nine siblings and not enough food for all of them to eat. Some of them were already running the streets themselves, like Maurice.

He went to a different elementary school than me and had family in the South (that's what we call the smaller cities to the south of Miami). When Maurice started at Drew with me, he was already ignorant and abrasive. He liked to humble me and my crew because he thought we were stuck-up. We couldn't even walk past him without him heckling us. "Y'all hoes think y'all all that!" He was annoying, always getting in trouble, and I had to curse him out on multiple occasions for being ignorant. One day he tried to beat up one of our teachers with a pipe and got sent to juvenile detention. I thought he was out of his mind. Maurice got arrested again when we were in high school for having drugs and guns on him, and when he was released a year or so later, he went right back to jail for attempted murder and had to do real prison time. It would be years until I saw him next. His was a lifestyle I had always been protected from, partly because my mom wanted to keep me safe, and partly because my dad was on the other side of it.

The drug game wasn't just creating more users; it was

birthing a generation of hustlers. It was risky business, but in the '80s and '90s, it was damn near inescapable in the hood. The only thing you could control was which side you would end up on. Our brothers, cousins, and fathers took risks that could get them killed, strung out, or locked up for the chance to take care of their families and finally be able to afford some luxuries in life. A lot of them lost, but some of them won. They weren't corporate businessmen, but they were smart and strategic. They were entrepreneurs, even if the money wasn't always legit. But with enough money and sense, they could transition into running legitimate businesses and stay off the radar.

I wasn't directly exposed to the drug game in my house. There was no scandal that exposed how my family's lifestyle was sustained. I just grew up. I paid enough attention to the rest of my environment that I could guess what the hushed conversations between adults around me were about. The guys who could afford brand-new Chevies and solid-gold teeth never went to any job but still had money.

Nessa always made sure I knew the code, even if I didn't know all the details. The first rule was minding my business. I knew not to ask too many questions about conversations and moves that didn't include me. Her logic was *If you don't see nothing, you can't know nothing, so there's nothing to talk about.* She never had to worry about anybody backing me into a corner to get any info, because I didn't have any to give. The older I got, the more I trusted my mother's judgment and guidance. Both Mr. Wonderful and my stepfather, Willie, were well-connected and respected in a network of moneymakers and shot-callers. Someone with allegiances to my family was always a stone's throw away, so my sister and I were protected without even knowing it. This safety was only guaranteed if we respected the rules and boundaries our parents laid out for us. It was a small price to pay for the comforts they provided us.

Chapter
2

The personal anthem of my childhood was undeniably "The Glamorous Life" by Sheila E. It seemed like she was the only woman in Prince's crew cool enough to stand next to him and be a pop star in her own right because this song was so amazing. It came out when I was still in elementary school, and whenever I caught the video on MTV, I stopped everything I was doing to watch it. I was enamored by the scenes of her riding around the city in a fur coat and making everyone's heads turn when she walked down the stairs of the club. It was such a flex. That was the lifestyle and the energy I wanted for myself. "The Glamorous Life" planted a seed that grew into an appreciation for opulence.

I looked forward to my eighth-grade prom for months because it was an opportunity for me to get all glammed up for an event. Unfortunately, my grandmother passed away the week before. It's a tradition in the Bahamas that when a loved one dies, you keep their body in the house for a few days so people can come see them when they pay their respects and say their final goodbyes before the burial. My entire family was shaken up by the loss of my grandmother, but my mom wanted to make sure that Stella and I didn't have to miss prom. We got our hair done and put on dresses with poufy sleeves. Our entire family was there before we got in the limousine to go, including my grandmother, who was lying in her casket in the living room. I chuckle remembering how fancy I felt and how excited I was for a dance while mourning with my family. It was proof that sadness and happiness can coexist.

A few months later, before I started high school, Fifteenth Avenue was full of even more commotion than usual in front of Mr. Wonderful's store: 2 Live Crew was shooting a music video for their song "Move Somethin'." The hip-hop group was the pride of Miami because their leader, Uncle Luke, was a popular DJ and promoter in the city before they blew up. They were demonized in the media because their lyrics were considered vulgar and too explicit for the general public, but the controversy only raised their profile and drew more fans to their music. The success of the group allowed Uncle Luke to start a record label, an underground radio station, and several other businesses. He was one of the city's movers and shakers, which meant he knew my dad well enough to use his corner store as the set for one of 2 Live Crew's videos.

My sister and I were beyond excited to have behind-the-scenes access to a music video set. But there were limitations. Nessa was familiar with the group's music and didn't want us fully exposed to whatever antics they might have planned, so she banished us to the back room of the store where we wouldn't be in the way. We heard the up-tempo song blaring from the speakers outside, the director calling out different commands on his loudspeaker, and the sounds of people hooting, hollering, and laughing. The biggest moment of the summer was unfolding just feet away from us, and the temptation was too much to bear. We had to see some of it for ourselves. The store was closed for the shoot, so there wasn't anyone inside. We snuck down one of the aisles and got as close to the glass door as we could without anyone noticing from outside. No one was paying attention, so we crept even closer, and I could see more of what was happening on the street. A half dozen women in short, tight outfits with high-heeled shoes and perfectly done-up hair were standing around. Their makeup accentuated their beauty, and they wore gold chains and sunglasses that made them look rich and bougie. I watched them talk and throw their heads back in laughter with effortless seductiveness. As soon as the music started again and the director yelled "Action!" they did a choreographed dance to the beat. The guys standing around went crazy, cheering and whistling.

I couldn't blame them, because even I was hypnotized. They were the stars of the show. Even though it was 2 Live Crew's video, those girls made it worth watching. They commanded so much attention and admiration. At that moment, they were the absolute center of the universe. It was inspiring to watch them influence the space and transform our little store into the hottest spot in the city for a few hours. They were bad in the best way possible. I tried to imagine what it felt like to hold that much power over a crowd just like Sheila E. did in the video for "The Glamorous Life." That's probably what I was fantasizing about when Nessa caught my sister and me snooping and snapped, "What did I tell y'all?!" We sulked back to our designated area, but I'd seen enough.

The same year, Eddie Murphy's *Coming to America* was released. It was one of the biggest movies of the year, and I loved it. The fictional royal family was surrounded by luxury and beauty, even when they arrived in New York City from Zamunda. The city looked like a completely different planet to me onscreen, with scenes of snow falling from the sky, steam and smoke rising from the ground, and millions of people living in it. All I knew were palm trees and bright bungalow houses growing up in Miami and the Caribbean. There were tall buildings downtown, but nothing like the cluster of skyscrapers and concrete I saw in *Coming to America*. I could accept the fantasy elements of a royal family, but I couldn't wrap my head around what parts of New York were real and what was made up for the movie. When Nessa told me the Waldorf Astoria, where King Jaffe and Queen Aoleon stayed, was a real hotel, I couldn't believe it. I developed a fixation with New York and nagged her about visiting for months. She promised to take me for our next family trip.

For my birthday that year, Laura; Nessa; our new stepdad, Willie; and one of my mom's friends were all with me when I took my first plane ride to the Big Apple. I stared out of the taxi window after we landed and was just as shook as Prince Akeem when he arrived in Queens. The buildings really did merge into one huge shape in the air. All of it was real, but the electricity of the city still felt magical. We visited the Statue of Liberty, the World Trade Center (when the Twin Towers were still standing), and the top of the Empire State Building. That's how I learned that clouds are like smoke, not something solid you can sit on or touch. We even stayed at the iconic Waldorf Astoria. When I got back to school, I couldn't wait to tell my friends that I had been to an actual concrete jungle and had my own *Coming to America* experience.

When I started ninth grade at Miami Northwestern Senior High School, I felt like I was closer to being the beautiful, confident woman I aspired to be. My thick thighs, hips, and booty had grown in. I was (and still am) notoriously small chested, but there wasn't any doubt in my mind that I was fine. Nessa kept my hair done, letting me try different styles like asymmetrical curls and ponytails with teased bangs. I was always in fly gear, down to shoes and accessories. Distressed-denim jeans, matching windbreaker sets—I had it all. I wore a wrist full of gold bangle bracelets that jingled with every step I took. You couldn't tell me I wasn't fresh.

Just like my elementary and middle schools, Miami

Northwestern was within walking distance of my Liberty City home base. Pinkey and I were still best friends, and we still walked home together. Now we took our time, trying to see and be seen as we strolled. It was part of our normal routine to take detours to talk to friends or stop at one of the hole-in-the-wall restaurants for conch fritters, plantains, or ice-cold sodas when it was hot outside. I felt untouchable because I was mature enough to understand the status I had as Mr. Wonderful's daughter. But I was still naïve enough to underestimate the unpredictability of the streets. You never knew what hand it was going to deal you, no matter how many rules you followed. And there were always wild cards in the deck. When people around you were starving, having food on your plate could put a target on your back, and I learned that the hard way.

One day after school during freshman year, Pinkey and I were on our normal stroll home. I noticed a guy on the other side of the street keeping the same pace as us. He made me uneasy, but I couldn't figure out why, so I wrote the feeling off. *Maybe he wants to holler at one of us and get our number*, I thought to myself. He wasn't smiling or trying to get our attention, though. We kept walking, and I turned my attention back to Pinkey. Before I had a chance to check if he was still walking on the opposite side, he was standing in front of us with a gun pointed our way. In a split second, so many scenarios went through my mind. *What if he forces us into a car and kidnaps us? What if I try to run and he shoots me in the back? Maybe Pinkey and I can try to physically attack him, but he's prob-*

ably stronger than us, and he has a gun. What if he shoots both of us? Maybe I can try to talk him down. I don't know what to say. I was more terrified than I had ever been in my life, and I was stuck. He reached for my bracelets with his free hand, and the movement broke my frozen trance. It gave me a moment of clarity: This was a stickup, and I was his mark. My only way out of this situation was to give him what he wanted. I couldn't stomach the thought of him coming any closer to me with the gun, so in one swift motion, I slid every bangle off my wrist, flinging them in his direction. The sound of them hitting and rolling on the concrete might as well have been a gunshot at the beginning of a track meet. Without saying a word, Pinkey and I took off running. I didn't look back to see if he was following us or stop to catch my breath until I made it to my mother's shop.

I burst into the salon breathless and trembling. My mouth was so dry I could barely speak. Her clients were so surprised and confused that they stared at me like I was the one holding a gun. As soon as I made eye contact with Nessa, I broke down crying and could barely stand. She rushed to make sure I was okay and figure out what was wrong. Through sobs, I told her what happened. She stiffened up, indignant and furious, and immediately got on the phone. I was still coming down from shock and adrenaline, so I didn't know who she was talking to, but I recounted the details as she asked me to. I spent the rest of the evening in the shop with her where I felt safe while she finished tending to her clients. For the remainder of the academic year, my mother made sure one of my aunts, uncles, or neighbors picked me up from school. I never heard anything else about it, and I didn't see the man who robbed me ever again.

For the first time, the danger of Liberty City landed directly at my feet. It shook me to my core and permanently disrupted the sense of safety I grew up with. I couldn't rely on my family's reputation to keep me out of harm's way all the time. I had to play a part in protecting myself by being more aware of my surroundings and the people in them. My need to plan and control the details of my social outings went into overdrive. Whenever I got ready to go anywhere with friends, I ran through a mental list of possible worst-case scenarios. If I was rushed, my anxiety would shoot through the roof because being unprepared felt like I was exposing myself to danger. I was vigilant about who was around and preferred to be more of an observer, as opposed to the outgoing life of the party all the time.

That didn't stop me from going out, though. As a Caribbean and Miamian, being social and partying are in my DNA. Uncle Luke played such a huge role in this part of my coming-of-age. He and the Ghetto Style DJs revolutionized Miami's signature booty-bass style of music, and it was the soundtrack of my teenage years. Luke's crew would host parties for teenagers called Pac Jams. This is where kids from all over Miami came together to dance and turn up. Instead of alcohol, the Pac Jams sold juices, pickles, hot sausages, potato chips, and fries. There were no VIP sections, just local dance teams that had something to prove on the dance floor. If a Pac Jam was happening, it was the only place you wanted to be on the weekend. Luke threw the teen parties at different venues around the city until he opened his own spot called the Pac Jam Teen Disco on Fifty-Fourth and Twelfth.

Pac Jam weekends were a ritual for me and my friends. On Saturday afternoons, I started making phone calls to make the plan. First, I had to confirm attendance. *Is your mom letting you go? Did she give you the money to get in?* Then we had to lock down the logistics. *My mama said she can drop us off, but somebody else has to pick us up. Let's meet at my house. What time do you want to get there?* That part was important because if we arrived too early, we looked lame standing around an empty party. But we didn't want to miss anything, so we couldn't be too late. Once transportation was booked, we had to figure out the vibe. *We should all wear pink. Do you have anything cute?* Sometimes, one person couldn't swing it and we had to improvise. *What about purple? Does anyone else have something she can borrow?* When all the details were in place, we—usually me, Pinkey, Stella, and my other cousin Joy—could discuss other pressing matters. *Is the boy you like, or the girl you can't stand, going to be there? The dance team that lost last week is coming back; I can't wait to see what they're going to do.* After I made my calls, I pressed my outfit and laid it across the bed where I could see it, made sure my hair was perfect, and started to count the minutes before I could pump a few spritzes of body spray on and head out.

My stomach fluttered with excitement whenever I walked into the dimly lit room, and not just because there were always a few guys checking me out. The Pac Jams were one of the few places I was allowed to go without adult supervision. It was full of kids from different neighborhoods and schools, so I got to be around new people who didn't immediately recognize me as Mr. and Mrs. Wonderful's daughter. I got to experience true independence where I could express myself and navigate situations how I wanted to. If I had problems with anybody, my crew and I could handle it on our own, instead of having to call in reinforcements. I could flirt and dance with boys without worrying if someone was going to report everything back to my family. I never knew what the night would bring, but the freedom of being mysterious was so exciting.

Like a lot of kids in the '80s, I naturally gravitated toward hip-hop. As a girl, seeing women like Queen Latifah and MC Lyte do their thing was special. MC Lyte was the first female rapper to make a solo album, and she was spitting with the same energy and flow as men like Rakim. She let it be known that a girl could keep up with the dudes in rap. Queen Latifah was smart, Afrocentric, and she always made songs from the perspective of women. Me and my girls knew all the words to "Ladies First" with Monie Love. The group Salt-N-Pepa was my absolute favorite, though. Queen Latifah and MC Lyte were dope rappers from the North who were tough and militant. Salt-N-Pepa was also from New York, and they wore baggy clothes but took it to a different level. They would rock oversized jackets or ripped jeans with tight bodysuits in bright colors. They ushered in the era of asymmetrical haircuts and set a whole new fashion trend. They're part of the reason I couldn't give up my big door-knocker earrings or gold chains, even after I was robbed. They weren't afraid to be playful, and their music was more upbeat and fun. They talked about sex in a way that was suggestive instead of explicit, and as a teenager I couldn't get enough of them.

I begged Nessa to let me go to the Salt-N-Pepa concert when they came to town. Pinkey and I were so excited when we finally got the tickets. I was the shortest one in my crew, just like Salt, so I wanted to dress like her. I wore a shiny spandex one-piece with a big multicolor racer jacket over it, even though it was hot as hell in Miami. My hair was cut short on one side and long on the other. Nessa couldn't take us and sent one of her friends to accompany us in the big crowd. Salt-N-Pepa looked just as stylish and sexy in person when they stepped onto the stage. We were so hyped! We rapped along to every word at the top of our lungs. They knew how to work the crowd and kept us out of our seats for the entire show. They were amazing performers.

As for me, I learned how to perform on a football field. Marching bands are a big deal in the South, especially at historically Black colleges and universities. If you've ever seen *Stomp the Yard*, you know what I mean. The tradition and competitiveness showcased at the college level often start at local high schools, especially in a football-focused environment like Liberty City, the neighborhood known for producing future NFL players. Chad "Ochocinco" Johnson, Amari Cooper, and Devonta Freeman were all once Liberty City kids, playing for local teams. During pauses in the game, marching bands and majorettes keep the crowd entertained with live music and dancing. Our high school games were always packed with people of all ages who didn't want to miss any of the action from the Mighty Marching Bulls.

I knew I wanted to be a majorette. There were cheerleading and competitive dance teams at my high school, but I didn't like how technical and acrobatic their style was. Those teams also required way too much practice, and I didn't want to sacrifice my social life. I didn't know how to play any instruments, so I wasn't joining the band. The flagettes were boring, so that was out, too. My mind was made up, but I had to wait until I was a sophomore to audition. I had several batons around the house—one with ribbons on the ends and one that lit up—that were old Christmas gifts. My uncle Perry, one of my mom's gay guy friends, knew how to twirl the baton and helped me get better at it. Auditions were held in the middle of the summer when it was scorching hot, and the process took all week. Everyone trying out had to learn a huge group routine, which was the most fun. The solo routine was more intimidating because that was the moment to really show the coaches and captains what you could do. I clearly impressed the leads because I made the team.

I loved being a majorette. It was so satisfying to see how our drills came together after weeks of practice. The band got their musical numbers down, then our majorette coaches helped us create choreography that added sass and seduction to the whole performance. We put on a hell of a show in the stands, on the sidelines, and at midfield during halftime.

When the announcers introduced us, we strutted out in our blue-and-gold uniforms on beat, and crowds in the hundreds went crazy with cheering and screaming. We learned how to rely on vibrations from the drumline and signals from our captain to stay on cue because it was too loud to hear anything else. It was on the field where I learned to let my starlight shine. In tights and rayon, with floodlights beaming on me, I could be louder, bolder, and more flirtatious than I was in real life.

Chapter

3

Dating wasn't something that preoccupied my mind a lot when I was young. A boy whose name I don't remember had a crush on me in sixth grade, and I made the mistake of giving him my phone number. When he called, Nessa gave me the benefit of the doubt that he only wanted to talk about something school related. After about two minutes, she realized he just wanted to talk to me, and she told me to end the call and stop tying up her phone line. I didn't understand why I couldn't carry on a conversation with him as I did with my girlfriends, so I asked her. She responded with a trivial, almost-mocking tone.

"How old is he?"

I admitted that he was the same age as me, and in that same tone, she followed up. "What could you all possibly have to talk about for so long at that age?" Then she got serious and added, "Anything he says in a conversation longer than five minutes is probably a lie." She wasn't making a judgment about his character or personality; it's just that he was a kid. Nessa knew that meant he didn't have the life experience, maturity, or common sense to hold a serious conversation about most things, especially not having a boo.

This was also around the time when my mother's salon replaced Mr. Wonderful's store as one of my and Laura's favorite spots to hang out. Laura liked it because she was also interested in styling, so she was learning the techniques. I liked it because I could eavesdrop on the adult conversations the women had with each other and with my hilarious uncle Perry, who also worked there. The salon clients were fly girls who reminded me a lot of my mom and aunts because they were just as beautiful and confident. I had so much respect for them. I learned how to sit quietly and pretend I wasn't listening while they spilled the tea, but I was hanging on to every word. They talked about everything: their jobs, their family drama, money, and of course, their relationships—the men they were dating; the men who wanted to date them; the men they wanted to date; the men they were married to, used to be married to, or who were married to someone else.

What I learned was that the specific details of a situation didn't matter as much as how a woman chose to handle it. I picked up on how the ladies responded to each other when talking about their relationships, and whether they approved of one another's choices. Affirmative head nodding or being interrupted by *I know that's right!* meant she'd done the right thing. If she was getting short answers or people were mumbling under their breaths, they thought she'd made a misstep. I'd get confirmation as soon as the unlucky lady left the shop and everyone else stopped holding their tongues. *Couldn't be me!* was all I needed to hear to know she took a tremendous "L."

What the women in my life taught me about men is that keeping your dignity and respect intact is the top priority. The worst thing you can do in a relationship is lose yourself so much that you allow someone to disrespect or disregard you. Men hold a lot of power in the world and in the lives of their women, so women have to be discerning about who has access to their time and attention. I learned that men show women that they're special and appreciated with actions, not words. If a man truly loves you, you should have something to show for it. My mom was my first example of this.

Nessa and Mr. Wonderful separated just as I was starting middle school. Moving from Aventura to central Miami was the only clue that something was changing in our family dynamic. Our parents' separation wasn't a life-altering event for Laura and me, and that was by design. We never saw any fights, arguments, or big blowups between them. Mr. Wonderful didn't live in the new house with us, but his presence in our lives was just as strong. We saw him pretty much every day. We kept our free access to the store, he still had family dinners with us, took us out, and celebrated holidays with us. Mr. Wonderful was so committed to his family that he never officially divorced my mom. He had veteran benefits that he wanted my mom to receive. She was the only woman he ever really loved, and he didn't trust anyone else to handle his affairs in life or after. He respected her enough to support her moving on, and she handled that process with just as much grace.

One night I came across pictures of my mom posing with a man I didn't recognize at a live Eddie Murphy show. (This was post-*Delirious* but pre-*Raw*.) From the way they were hugged up, she clearly knew him well. When I asked her about him, she just smiled and said he was a friend. It was at least another year before I finally met Willie, the man who would become my stepfather. All my family was gathered for a party, and he came up to introduce himself. He clearly knew more about me and Laura than we knew about him, but he was easygoing and funny as hell. After the initial introduction, we mostly saw him in passing, when he was picking Nessa up or dropping her off. Mr. Wonderful was a bit older than my mom, but Willie was closer to her age. It was cute to see her be so energetic and hip. My stepfather got bonus points because he was also from the Bahamas, and he even had a stamp of approval from Mr. Wonderful himself. Whenever they were in the same space, they shook hands and embraced each other as friends. Mr. Wonderful was kind of a mentor to my stepfather, and it helped make the transition easier for everyone.

The peace that my mother was able to maintain in her old and new relationships was not lost on me. She always handled herself with grace and hardly ever got out of character. That's how she earned the respect of so many people around her. She knew how she wanted to be treated and never settled. Her children were always her priority, and no matter what happened in her relationships, she was going to make sure we were safe and taken care of. She only tolerated partners who could support and encourage that.

I didn't need my mother to warn me about the dangers of falling in love with the wrong person, because I was seeing it happen around me. I knew girls who got pregnant in high school and found out the hard way that the love they thought their boyfriends had for them wasn't real. I saw how some guys liked to control women by making them feel insecure and stripping them of their sense of self. Nessa made it a point to remind my sister and me that we were beautiful and worthy, so we didn't have to seek that validation from anyone else. However, she knew from personal experience that being beautiful wouldn't stop a man from being disloyal or trying to take advantage of you. She never bashed my biological father to me, but Nessa always reminded me that her being beautiful and strong didn't stop him from walking away from both of us when she was pregnant. Being beautiful would only get me so far. I had to be smart, honor my opinions and beliefs first, and not give anyone the power to turn my life upside down.

My vision for what a relationship should look like was shaped by the women I saw around me. Their men bought them designer clothes, took them on trips, helped them open businesses, and treated them to dates out on the town. At the very least, my parents already made sure I didn't want for anything, so that's what I expected when I was old enough to date. So even though a few of my classmates liked me, I didn't think a high school boy could keep up with my standards.

Big M lived around the corner from my mom's house in central Miami. We met when I was fourteen. He was older than me by a few years. He'd already graduated from high school, and I liked that about him. He went out of his way to talk to me whenever he saw me, and I liked that he was more mature than the guys I went to school with. He was cute, too. Because I wasn't allowed to "entertain" boys at that age, he couldn't come inside the crib or call me too often. So he would sit in our front yard, keeping me company and talking for hours. He made me feel like one of his equals, even though I was younger than him and still in school. These conversations helped our friendship, and our mutual crush, grow over time. Even Nessa grew to like him after a while.

Big M jokingly called me his girlfriend a few times, but I never took him seriously, because I knew he was dating a girl closer to his age. I never met her, but people who knew us both always commented that she and I looked alike. Big M was very open and honest, so he never hid his relationship status from me. His girlfriend was old enough to spend time with him. He was allowed to go inside of her house, and they were definitely sexually active. I was too young to be in his life romantically. We remained innocent neighborhood friends for years, even though we both wanted something more.

A couple of years into our friendship, Big M broke up with

his girlfriend. Once I turned sixteen and my mom allowed me to date, he asked me to be his girlfriend, and I said yes. It's what we'd both wanted for a while. The transition from friends to lovers was easy because we knew each other so well. My classmates thought it was cool that I had an older boyfriend with a car who could take us wherever we wanted to go. Nessa approved of him and got to know his family, so she was comfortable with us spending more time together. I liked how grown I felt when he picked me up from school or after games when I had to perform with the majorette team. Once we were a couple, he was protective and sweet in a way he couldn't be when we could only talk in my yard. I enjoyed getting to know that side of him. He made me feel special and went from my neighborhood crush to the first boy I ever fell in love with.

Within a few months, things started getting more physical between us. Big M evolved from wrapping his arm around my shoulders and planting light kisses on my lips to tonguing me down while he rubbed my butt. I didn't mind. One day, we went to eat at Red Lobster and had the place to ourselves when we got back to Big M's. We were doing our normal thing, kissing and carrying on, but this time was different. He was kissing me deeper and touching me in places he hadn't touched me before. I knew he wanted to have sex. I did, too. But now that it was right in front of me, I panicked. Immediately, I recalled stories my friends told me about losing their virginities, and none of them were good. They said "popping your cherry" is painful and bloody. I wasn't prepared for any of that. All of a sudden, I had all the sex questions in the world. So I paused our fooling-around session and suggested we eat some of our leftover lobster. That gave me a chance to call Nessa.

"I think something is about to happen," I explained. "I don't know what to do."

She didn't try to talk me out of it. She just asked me a loaded question. "Are you sure this is something you want to do?"

It was. I loved Big M, and I enjoyed the physical connection we'd been building. I trusted him to be the first person I shared a full sexual experience with. Knowing that my mind was made up, Nessa answered my questions about what to expect. She confirmed that it might be painful and that I should pay attention to my body telling me I might not be ready for full penetration yet. She said my friends were exaggerating about the blood. She told me not to, under any circumstances, do anything without a condom. I hung up the phone reassured and returned to my date night ready to let the events unfold.

Big M picked up where we had left off, and I followed his lead. He undressed me with a carefulness I'd never seen from him before. I didn't feel uncomfortable letting him see my body. As he hovered over me on the bed, my thoughts raced with anticipation. It was like I was being let in on the biggest secret, but I was also making it happen. I was still a little nervous but more excited than anything else. He was on top of me in his bed, and I lay there trying to predict what sex would feel like. I waited for the moment to come when I crossed over into "not virgin" territory and saw the world in a whole different way. He pressed against me, gently at first, hoping to glide in.

It wasn't working. He tried again, this time with more force, and it hurt like hell. I gave him another chance to get it right, and that time hurt even worse, so we stopped. It went just like Nessa said it might. He made sure I was okay as we got dressed. I was—I just felt awkward and a little disappointed that I had to go home still a virgin. I told Nessa what happened, and I could see the *told you so* smirk on her face. She didn't judge me, though. She was satisfied knowing that I decided to go there with Big M on my terms and not his. Within a couple of weeks of our first attempt, Big M and I got it right.

We'd been together for over a year when Big M broke the news to me that he was moving to Atlanta. He wanted to start a new life for himself somewhere fresh. It was the beginning of the '90s in Miami, with drugs and gangs still going strong. There were only a handful of routes out of that lifestyle, and Big M wanted to take one of the better ones. I understood why he was leaving, but it hurt to see him go. I loved Big M. I was used to seeing him every day, and I was going to miss him dearly. We promised each other the distance didn't mean the end of our relationship, and for a little while, we meant it.

I started senior year of high school with a long-distance boyfriend. Big M and I talked on the phone every single day. I kept him updated on my life at school and in our neighborhood. He told me about his job hunt and plans to get settled in Georgia. We often shared how much we missed each other, and he kept suggesting that I come visit. That was out of the question. Yes, my mother trusted my judgment and allowed me to have a lot of independence as a young lady in my teens. Yes, she knew Big M and I were sexually active. Yes, she chose to support me through that experience instead of trying to stop me and running the risk of me doing it in secrecy. But I was still her underage high school daughter, and she was not giving me permission to fly out of town to visit my boyfriend in another city. I knew better than to even ask her. But Big M didn't drop it, and the longer we were apart, the more I wanted to see him. I knew my mother would never let me go, so I decided not to ask her.

I looked up flights and roped Pinkey into yet another one of my schemes: a day trip to Atlanta. Everything went smoothly with our quick morning flight. Big M picked us up from the airport and showed us around the city. We went to the mall and ate at a really good soul-food restaurant. He was living with relatives in a nice, spacious house in the Stone Mountain suburb. He drove us to see the mountain the city was named after, and it was the first time I'd seen such a beautiful landscape. Pinkey and I weren't ready to leave when he had to drive us to the airport for our return flight, but we had to be back in Miami before Nessa suspected anything.

Before we went through security, we learned that our flight was delayed. I wasn't too worried, because it was still early enough for us to have a little wiggle room. We left the airport to have dinner before we flew out and when we returned, the flight was delayed even more. It was time to worry. Then it was delayed again. My stomach dropped. We weren't scheduled to land in Miami until two in the morning. I had no choice but to call my mom and tell her where we were.

"This is what happens when you lie to me. It can blow up in your face just that quick."

That's all Nessa had to offer before she hung up and went to sleep. I knew I was in a shitload of trouble when I got home, but spending time with Big M and Pinkey in a new city for a few hours was worth it.

Chapter

4

Growing up, I often found myself drawn to architecture and real estate, a personal interest probably passed down from my grandfather. Before starting a family, General Archibald Taylor worked for the Crown (the official head of state) in Bermuda and the Bahamas as a builder. He owned property in the Bahamas, but like so many Caribbeans, he knew there were even more opportunities in the United States. Miami is only thirty minutes from the Bahamas by plane, but my grandfather arrived by boat. He initially set himself up in Overtown, a mostly Black neighborhood that many immigrants called home until the '50s when I-95 was constructed right through it. He put his skills to use and built the Taylor house in Liberty City from the ground up with his bare hands.

He died before I was born, but my grandfather is probably

why I loved any opportunity to drive past the huge mansions in Miami's affluent neighborhoods. We'd take weekend trips to Haulover Beach, riding past pristine homes sittin' right on the coast. I stared at each structure, curious about who lived there, what they did for a living, and all the decisions and steps that went into the design and construction—the placement of the windows, the wood used to make staircase railings, or how the garage was attached to the rest of the house. All of it fascinated me. When I learned that architects were the people who brought properties into being, I thought that's what I wanted to be when I grew up. The older I got, the more it seemed like a pipe dream. I didn't learn about architecture in school, and any time an architect was mentioned, it was never a woman, let alone a Black woman. My interest in properties never left, but architecture stopped being a career aspiration of mine when I realized it was a specialized field that required a degree and years of specific training.

College was never prioritized in my household as the only route to success. Most of the people around me were hustlers—either entrepreneurs, street cats, or both. They spent a few months learning a trade like carpentry and went into business for themselves, or they got a job and worked their way up, or they got money illegally. Either way, they made sure they had the money to get what they wanted: New cars. Apartments. Clothes for them and their kids. Jewelry. Anybody who wasn't going out and making it happen for themselves was struggling. I had a deep desire to be a powerful, independent woman who could stand on her own and have the finest things in life. That was *my* definition of a bad bitch. There was no doubt that I would make it, even if I didn't know how.

I always thought college made the most sense for people who were incentivized to go. An athletic scholarship or a guaranteed job after the completion of the degree seemed like hustles that made college worth it. I was a decent student in high school and didn't struggle to pull good grades in any subject that I was interested in and put effort into, but I wasn't what anyone would call a passionate learner. I wouldn't have passed a single semester of college if I only went because I thought it was the next step after high school, and Nessa made it clear that she wouldn't foot the bill for higher education if I wasn't locked in and focused. By the time I was a senior in high school, a diploma felt like more of a formality, one of the necessary steps I had to take because I was under-age. I was most passionate about making my own money, and I didn't think I needed four more years of studying and tests to achieve that.

Plus, Pinkey and I had the party bug bad in the early '90s. Every weekend, and sometimes on weekdays, we found ourselves out late. We went to house parties, club let outs, pretty much anywhere that let us in. We didn't even need fake IDs for the eighteen-and-older spots if we wore the right outfits and smiles. The only thing standing in the way of our good times was school: 7:30 a.m. start times, homework, and finals meant we couldn't stay out all night, every night. High school was fine, especially when it was football season and I was most active with the majorettes, but it wasn't special. I attended senior prom with my cousin Stella, which was fun, but it didn't feel significant, because mentally, I was already done with high school and looked forward to the last day.

Unfortunately, I hit a major roadblock when I had a mandatory meeting with the guidance counselor to go over my transcripts and make sure I was set to graduate. I was a class credit short of fulfilling the requirements to get a degree because I'd failed another science class. I struggled with the subject from ninth through twelfth grade. I never thought I needed to know anything about science in my life outside of school, so I never committed to trying to do well. The final straw was when I walked into the first day of biology in twelfth grade and the dead frogs were waiting for us on trays, ready to be dissected. It freaked me out, and I just never went back to class. I hoped the rest of my grades and overall GPA would be enough for me to earn my diploma anyway, but that was wishful thinking. Not graduating wasn't an option, though. Nessa would have kicked my ass, and after four years of hard work, I felt like I'd earned my spot to walk across that stage. I pleaded with my science teacher and administrators to give me an opportunity to earn the credits I needed. It was too late in the year for me to make the class up without having to re-enroll the next school year. Summer school was the only option. While everyone else was finally free from academic responsibilities, I had to attend several weeks of classes before I could graduate. I was pissed, but I begrudgingly got it done and got my diploma.

I didn't throw a graduation party or anything. Pinkey,

Stella, and the rest of my crew just kept the turn-up going with a new sense of freedom. Even though I was only seventeen, I no longer had to worry about the constraints of school nights. The week I was finally done with summer classes, Pinkey and I went to a party at a lounge. I had my hair in an updo with a tight dress on, and my lip gloss and liner were popping. It was another epic night of dancing and celebrating. "Baby Got Back" had just come out, and it was an anthem for us thick girls, so I was definitely letting loose. We left as the party spilled outside and took our time walking back to our car. We played it cool as guys sized us up while we switched by, and I felt one of them gently grab my arm. I looked up at a tall, milk-chocolate-complected man with a gold grill in his mouth that said HOLLYWOOD. I could tell his parted haircut was fresh. He was fine as hell. His touch was smooth and confident, but he had a laid-back swagger that made me want to know everything about him. I was instantly drawn to his energy. I gave him my phone number and looked forward to hearing from him.

.... ◆ ....

Within a few weeks of finishing school, I got my first job answering phones and doing administration work at an insurance company. It was so boring, but I was so happy to be earning my own money. They offered me $800 every two weeks, and I was eager to put it to work. I didn't think $1,600 a month was going to make me rich, but I assumed it was more than enough for me to live alone. As soon as I knew the job was mine, I set my sights on a place. My mom owned a beautiful three-bedroom house, complete with a lawn. It was one of her investment properties, and I knew it was still unoccupied. The rent was $800, only half of my new monthly income. One room would be my bedroom, the other would be a closet, and the third one could be a guest room, or more closet space. My imagination was already running wild.

"Are you sure you're ready to take on that kind of responsibility?" Nessa asked me when I told her I wanted to move in.

I didn't understand why she was being so hesitant, and I insisted I could handle it. She didn't seem convinced, but she agreed to let me rent the house. She turned serious, with an all-about-business tone: "The rent must get paid every month. This is not up for debate or discussion, and it has nothing to do with me bringing you into this world."

Well, damn. That's what I thought to myself, but all I said out loud was "I understand." I was too giddy to make my dreams of independence come true. I felt like a million bucks when I moved in with my bedroom furniture from my mom's. At seventeen, I was the only one of my friends who had their own crib. I was already getting a head start on the boss life I wanted.

Then the bills started to come in. On top of the rent, I had to pay for cable service, phone service, yard services to keep the lawn up to code, and electricity. That brought my monthly housing expenses closer to $1,000 a month. I also had to have food, toiletries, and cleaning supplies. That brought me to $1,200 a month. Up to that point, I had only ever counted and spent money, not worked for it or managed any of my own. Not only had I underestimated how much living on my own would cost, but I also hadn't realized my checks would be subject to taxes and cut down to $600 every two weeks. That left me with just enough money to pay for rent, utilities, and essentials, and not a single thing more.

With Nessa's warning about the rent ringing in my head, I knew I had to figure something out. I needed a job that paid more. My godsister Angie was doing customer service at an AT&T call center and suggested that I apply. She vouched for me, and I was offered a position right away, so I quit the insurance company job. After making it through training and my first couple of weeks at AT&T, I was so relieved that my paycheck was over a hundred dollars more than the ones at my last job. I was able to pay all the bills as they came, instead of picking which ones I could afford in the moment. But I still couldn't splurge on new outfits and go out every single weekend, even though I tried. I would pull up to my mother's house to get good home-cooked meals instead of having to stock my own refrigerator if it meant I could keep my social life going. Unfortunately, the penny-pinching couldn't stop me from falling behind on rent. I had to accept that I was stuck and fucked.

This was not the life of comfortable independence that I had imagined for myself, but I had too much pride to bow out gracefully. I tried not to mention the unpaid rent in hopes that Nessa would show me some grace, or that I would figure something else out in the meantime. She let me slide for the first month I didn't pay. When two months passed without the debt being settled, she told me I had to get out. I stayed put for a week to call her bluff in case she was just trying to scare me. Would my mother actually kick me out of my crib? The answer was yes. I was back in my room at her house before two months of past due rent turned into three.

Fumbling my first rental helped me let go of this fantasy I had that shit would just work out for me because I wanted it to. I needed a plan for how I was going to achieve whatever I wanted to have in life. I had no clue how many hours of grinding, how many failures, and how much "figuring it out" women like my mom and aunts had to do. But I would eventually find out.

Chapter

5

Hollywood started calling me the same week we met. He took me out to eat for our first date, and we hit it off instantly. We talked for hours, and I was so impressed to learn that he and his best friend, Ted Lucas, were big-time promotors who hosted parties and concerts all over the city. They brought acts like Frankie Beverly & Maze and Earth, Wind & Fire to perform. Ted wanted to get even deeper into the entertainment industry and had started building the record label of his dreams: Slip-N-Slide Records. Hollywood was loyal to him and planned on sticking by Ted's side to make sure it was a success. Hollywood was intelligent, charismatic, and respected in the streets. Knowing that I could attract guys like this, who were making big moves, made me feel accomplished in my own right. I felt like

I was headed in the right direction by surrounding myself with people who were ambitious and successful.

After that first date, Hollywood and I kept talking on the phone, but we didn't see each other again for a while. I made it clear to him that I didn't want to be in a relationship. Big M and I never officially split, but the distance started to take its toll, especially now that I was out of high school and living life in Miami. It was harder for us to keep each other's attention, and our calls grew less and less frequent, but I wasn't in a rush to replace him. Then, a few weeks after we met, Hollywood got into a motorcycle accident and broke his leg. We talked to each other on the phone often as friends, but I understood my role as someone new in his life. We had only seen each other in person a couple of times, so I wasn't comfortable making myself available to him while he was healing from a big injury. That was something his family, close friends, or maybe a girlfriend should be doing. I wanted to spend time with him, but I played it cool by not being too eager. Neither my nonchalance nor his broken leg stopped Hollywood from blowing my phone up and eventually coming to see me at my mother's shop. He literally hobbled in with his leg in a cast one day. He was clearly a charmer. He had everybody in the salon, including Nessa, cracking up with his jokes and banter. My mom liked him right away and thought he was one of the funniest people ever. He kept calling, showing up, bringing me gifts, and letting it be known that he was serious about wanting to be with me. Once I realized that he wasn't just trying to put me in a rotation of women he was dating, I agreed to be his girlfriend, and we were locked in. Things between Big M and me naturally fizzled out, and it was understood that we'd both moved on.

Hollywood could be super silly when he wanted to be, but he also knew how to make people feel like they were the most important person in the room. He made eye contact when you talked to him, and he spoke with so much confidence it was like he was pouring into you. He didn't just win me over; he won Nessa and Laura over, too. As we spent more time together, my mother would take his side over mine in our petty squabbles. Hollywood was the first boyfriend that she ever allowed to stay over at our house. I made a good impression on his mom, too. He owned a house in Carol City, a few neighborhoods away from Liberty City. I spent most of my time there after I got evicted from Nessa's rental. When Hollywood's mom came to stay with him after her home was damaged by a hurricane, we got to bond, and she became really fond of me.

The most important mutual connection between Hollywood and me was revealed a few weeks after we started dating when I took an unplanned call. "I heard you messing with my brother!" Those were not the words I expected to hear when I reluctantly accepted a jail call from Maurice, the annoying boy from the Beans. Since going to prison for attempted murder, he had thrown himself into music and started writing raps under the name Trick Daddy Dollars. Whenever he could, he would spit his rhymes, talk shit, and get updates on the hood from whoever just so happened to answer his phone call. That's how he found out I was dating Hollywood, his half brother. I had no clue they were related. They had the same father—who had spawned something like fifteen kids—and different moms. Hollywood was raised in the South with his mom, while Trick was in Liberty City with his mom and nine other siblings. Plus, they couldn't be more different. Trick was harsh and tended to be reckless, but his brother was smooth and low-key. The only thing they really had in common was a daddy and the streets. Hollywood was known to keep a gun on him—the same thing that had landed Trick in jail. Once Trick found out that I was spending most of my time with his brother, I couldn't get rid of him.

Hollywood was one of the good things in my life that just fit perfectly. We looked great together and matched each other's fly everywhere we went. I loved the way I felt on his arm walking through the mall or at a football game. Whenever we would pass people, I felt like the envy of every woman, and I knew he was the envy of a lot of men who weren't discreet when they sized me up. This was my first relationship as a young adult, not a high schooler who still needed permission to go out, and it was with a man of my dreams. He filled in so many gaps during this part of my life. I still got to experience independent living by staying at his house instead of my mom's. He worked in the nightlife scene that my friends and I were always trying to be in. We clubbed together at spots like Paradise and Luke's Miami Beach, one of the adult clubs Uncle Luke opened. Hollywood spoiled me with gifts I didn't have to buy myself. Most importantly, he made me feel like a princess when we were together. He valued me, and I knew he had my back.

I didn't have any doubts that Hollywood and I would be together forever. There was nothing standing in the way of our relationship continuing to grow. We weren't talking about marriage, though. We actually had a healthy balance of independence from each other. He still did his own thing, hanging out with his friends—and probably flirting with other women—and so did I. Being on the scene was a core part of my identity back then. My friends and I all looked good and were on our way to becoming the hot girls in our city. The fun wasn't just in the music and dancing; we had a different kind of power. Being a beautiful woman is, and always has been, a form of currency. It can buy you things that money can't if you're confident enough to use it. You can feel that power when you walk into a room. Getting dressed to kill in skintight dresses or denim coochie-cutter short sets with halter tops was part of a ritual we looked forward to after work. We were the epitome of bad bitches, so we took every opportunity to show out.

In the years since "Move Somethin'," Uncle Luke was making music as a solo artist in addition to 2 Live Crew. His record label, Luke Records, was one of the first that focused on Southern hip-hop, which wasn't nearly as popular as it is today. Luke was a bona fide superstar and royalty in Miami. To me, he was like a play uncle because of his ongoing friendship with my parents. In the spring of 1993, I ran into one of my old classmates who was an amazing dancer. He was a member of one of the teams that tore the floor up at the Pac Jams. He told me that he was going to be in an Uncle Luke music video. His eyes lit up when he invited me. *You should come!* He was so excited to be in a music video, and I was right there with him. The memory of 2 Live Crew shooting "Move Somethin'" at my dad's store, and the women who were in it with them, was still fresh in my mind. I knew that Luke had a reputation for being nasty and wild, but I didn't want to do it for that. I wanted the opportunity to immortalize myself as young, beautiful, and part of what was popping.

Of course, I invited Pinkey to come along, and a couple of days later we pulled up to a huge mansion that sat right on Miami's Biscayne Bay. I couldn't get a true feel for the ambiance of the house because it was packed full of camera crews trying to get everything together. I was so relieved when I realized the video was for one of Luke's more innocent records, "It's Your Birthday." It's an up-tempo party track, but the video was still a classic Uncle Luke affair. There were a lot of women in bikinis, shaking their butts and popping them on full display. I knew I wasn't going to do all of that, because Luke was like family and it didn't seem appropriate. Plus, I hadn't even told Nessa I was going to a video shoot. No one gave us any instructions for what to do on camera, so I changed into my black swim top with shorts on the bottom and easily blended in with the other extras. I watched where everyone else was gathering and tried to find a spot where Pinkey and I could get some camera time but not be front and center. I hadn't seen Luke at all since I'd been there, and I didn't want to. I was scared he'd recognize me and kick me off the set.

Within a few minutes, I was completely comfortable because the shoot turned into a big party. I only remembered we were on camera when the director guided the crowd or yelled "Cut!" There's a part of "It's Your Birthday" where individual people get birthday shout-outs, and word spread around the party that the production crew was picking people to say their names into the camera. I didn't know if I would be chosen, but I secretly hoped I was, to get my few seconds of spotlight. The crew was getting closer to us and filmed a couple of other girls first, and then they came right toward me. They were moving super quick, so when they set me up for the shot, I didn't have time to be nervous. They told me all they needed was my name and to keep dancing as I said, "Trina!"

We stayed on set for the whole night and had so much fun. It was so packed inside that we left without Luke even knowing we were there. "It's Your Birthday" became one of Luke's most popular hits. For the next couple of weeks, I was super geeked to tell my friends that I was in the Luke video. I built up all this anticipation for it to come out so everyone could see me. They probably thought I had some major role, but I ended up getting less than two seconds of screen time, as long as it took me to say my name. When Luke saw me in the final cut, he reached out and said, "Your mother is going to kick my ass!" But he spared me the disappointment and kept my scene in the video anyway.

Finally being in a music video was just one of the highlights of my first year out of high school. Big M and I weren't together anymore, but it was because of him that I knew how cheap and convenient it was to fly from Miami to Atlanta. My crew and I made it our designated spot for a weekend getaway out of town. Between Freaknik and the HBCU homecomings, Atlanta was *the* place to party for young Black people in the '90s. Because there were so many college students, it didn't matter that we weren't twenty-one yet. We had faith that the same thing that got us into the spots in Miami would work there, too. We caught the flight, piled into a single hotel room, and let the vibes take us where they would. We didn't care about sharing beds, because we didn't plan on spending a lot of time in the room, and we didn't worry about slim pockets, because we could always find somebody to foot the bill. We got dolled up in our finest leather and denim—the fashions that defined the '90s—to hit the Lenox Square mall and go out to eat during the day, then club all night.

On one particular trip, we pulled up to a spot that was really popping and had a line snaking down the block. We hopped in line, determined to wait it out and get inside one way or another. We were finally close enough to see the entrance and the bouncers guarding it, when a big group of guys started heading straight toward the door. I couldn't believe my eyes when I realized who was in the crew: Tupac and Too $hort. A few people started screaming and yelling out to them, but

I instinctively knew not to overreact. My homegirls and I all looked at each other, and we were clearly on the same page. Without saying a word, we straightened our posture and settled into our best bad-bitch stances—looking confident and unbothered with our heads held high—as they got closer to the door and us. The timing was perfect because there were only two or three groups in front of us when one of the unrecognizable guys in the entourage started scoping out the honeys in the crowd. We offered coy smiles but nothing more. The honey trap was set.

He walked straight over to us. "Y'all are with us now." Then he put his arm around my shoulders and walked us in with the group. I didn't show it on my face, but internally I was beaming. The scene was hectic from the moment we stepped inside the club because as soon as the DJ announced that Too $hort and 'Pac were in the building, people started swarming their VIP section. Through all the chaos, my friends and I managed to make minor introductions to the superstars, but that was it. As much as we loved the thrill of being in the VIP with two of the hottest rappers, it was hard to enjoy ourselves with so many people being thirsty for their attention. We weren't groupies and weren't going to fight for a spot just to stand next to celebrities. It was enough that everyone saw us walk in with them. We held our ground in the VIP long enough to have a few drinks from their bottle, and then we excused ourselves to have our own fun.

Those years were some of the best of my life. I thought

I had everything I could possibly want: A family I was close with. Homegirls that would always ride for me and with me. A man who loved me and would do anything for me. I thought life would keep getting better from there. But that's not how life works.

Chapter 6

June 22, 1994, is one of the days that changed my life forever. The night before, Hollywood and I went out go-kart racing with one of our friends, Fatso. The two of them were thick as thieves, and Fatso never minded playing third wheel with us. I didn't complain, because hanging out with Hollywood's friends always made me feel safe and protected. I knew they moved carefully in the streets. As we left go-karting, Hollywood talked about plans for the rest of the night. He didn't offer any details, and I assumed I was joining them to keep our festivities going. When he told me he was dropping me off at home instead, I flat out told him no. I didn't want to sit at home alone while he was still out having fun. Fatso sat silently as Hollywood and I argued back and forth in Hollywood's Buick. I accused him of trying to sneak off to talk to other girls. He denied it and brushed me off but

didn't change his mind about taking me home. I resorted to
the silent treatment and ended up falling asleep before we
even made it to Nessa's. By this point, my pride kicked in,
and I refused to beg Hollywood to let me hang out with him
and his friend. I went in the house, sleepy and salty, and went
straight to bed.

The phone jolted me out of my sleep at around six in the
morning. One of Hollywood's sisters was on the other end,
shouting, "TURN ON THE NEWS RIGHT NOW!"

I fumbled for the remote, found the right channel, and focused on their report. My stomach dropped as I processed the
news. Two men had been killed in a drive-by shooting while
sitting in a Buick the same make and model as Hollywood's.

One of the men who had died on the scene was identified.
It was Fatso. My chest tightened.

I knew the other person had to be Hollywood, but I refused
to accept it until I was absolutely sure. I started dialing the
number to Hollywood's pager and house phone over and over,
hoping for an answer that never came. Desperate for information, one of my friends called the hospital that was mentioned
in the news report, where the unknown victim was taken. The
staff couldn't provide a lot of details about who it was, because
he had been shot so many times that his face was messed up.
But what they did tell her confirmed the worst. The unnamed
victim was wearing a gold grill that said HOLLYWOOD.

Everything went black for me.

Grief and shock took over like a dark fog that covered my
brain and body. I remember certain sensations in the hours

and days after finding out Hollywood was gone: swollen eyes from crying, my throat being scratchy from screaming, different arms around me trying to offer comfort that I couldn't receive. I remember sitting with Hollywood's mother, some of his siblings, and his friends. All of us were swimming in an ocean of hurt and confusion.

Trick, who was still in jail, called me after he found out. I heard nothing but pure pain and rage in his voice. Hollywood was his brother and his best friend. The department of corrections arranged for Trick to attend his brother's funeral, and Ted helped pay for the transport. Trick was escorted through the church by two armed guards, handcuffed and shackled the entire time. No one was allowed to touch or hug him. He tried to keep his composure and not let the devastation take over. It didn't feel right that Trick had to grieve his brother in that way. I felt frozen in disbelief and absolutely helpless during the service as I sat next to Hollywood's mother and sisters. I didn't think the tears would ever stop.

I knew the ugly truth of the streets, but this was the first time it ended up on my doorstep. When my grandmother died, I was hurt and missed her dearly. But she was older when she passed and had lived a full life. One moment Hollywood was with me, having the time of our lives, and the next moment he was gone. The person I spent most of my time with, the person I was so excited to watch do amazing things, the person I wanted to do amazing things with was taken away from me in the blink of an eye. The heartbreak was disorienting and all-consuming. I still had breath in my body, but my entire life felt like it had been ripped to pieces and scattered everywhere. I had no idea if it would ever be put back together, or how. I was floating on a cloud of light and highs before that, like anything was possible. Then I was plunged into the darkest place I'd ever been.

Chapter

7

I spent the rest of the summer and fall after Hollywood's murder trying to not think about everything that I had lost. I thought if I didn't acknowledge the dark cloud that was constantly over me, it didn't exist. I leaned into what I knew, what I was comfortable with: the fast party life. That was a world that still made sense to me. It was a space where I felt in control. The ritual of making myself over, listening to music that was so loud I couldn't hear my own thoughts, dancing in a room full of mostly strangers, and spending a few hours without the expectation of deep conversations or meaningful decisions was soothing. So that's what I did to take my mind off the turmoil I felt in my heart.

My birthday was coming up, and I wanted to do something that Hollywood and I had talked about when he was still alive. He and Ted had been putting on concerts in the city with acts that attracted a more mature, soulful crowd. The last one they put together before his passing included LeVert, Silk, and H-Town, but they hadn't sold as many tickets or made as much money as they wanted to. This letdown is part of why he pivoted to focus more on Slip-N-Slide. Because I'd grown up in the Pac Jams, where new Miami bass artists would try their music on the crowd and get brutally honest reactions about whether they were good or bad, I knew young people and hip-hop lovers were the most eager to see their performers live. I suggested that an event targeting them might have a better turnout. Even though Hollywood was gone, I wondered if I could still make it happen.

Ted was completely on board with the idea, and he helped me go about figuring out the venue and taking care of the up-front and overhead costs and deciding how to promote it. We booked three rap acts that were just starting to blow up, driven by growing fan bases that were ahead of the curve. Our head-liner was Da Brat. Her single, "Funkdafied," was tearing up the charts, and when her debut album dropped, she became the first solo female rapper to go platinum. She was being supported by two up-and-coming artists on Bad Boy Records. Craig Mack had one of the biggest singles of the year, "Flava in Ya Ear." It had the streets going crazy, and he'd dropped a remix with his labelmate, who we also booked to perform: Notorious B.I.G. His first album, *Ready to Die*, dropped in September of that year, and he was still promoting it when we reached out to his management.

For months, this was my passion project. I was constantly

on the phone with Ted and his guys getting updates on the venue, permits, ticket sales, and logistics. We secured the legendary Cameo Theater for the show, which made me feel so official knowing that so many famous acts had graced the stage. I wanted the event to happen in December to coincide with my birthday, but there were scheduling conflicts that forced us to push it back to January 21. I didn't even care. Nothing was going to stand in my way. There were advertisements in the newspapers and on the radio to promote the event. Once we sold enough tickets to cover everything and booked travel for all the performers, it was a done deal. I knew I'd pulled it off.

On the day of the show, we had a limousine booked to pick everyone up from the airport and get them to the venue. I rode along to pick up Craig Mack. He didn't have that many people with him, and I'll never forget how humble and nice that man was. I was prepared for him to be short and distant since he was a celebrity and I was a stranger, but he was beyond gracious and warm. He spoke to me with respect like I was his equal, not a fan or the help. He asked questions about the show and thanked me for having him. After we dropped him off at his hotel, I went back to the airport to grab Brat. She was more reserved and observant than Craig. I could tell by the way she hesitantly said "Nice to meet you?" that she was street-smart and savvy—you have to be, growing up in Chicago. She was probably expecting someone older and male to be coordinating the logistics for her show (because it's a male-dominated field) and was trying to figure out who I was and how I ended up in that limo with her. I didn't take it personally. With her signature braids and swag, she seemed like one of the coolest, most mysterious women I'd ever met. It's been almost twenty years since that day, and whenever I see her, Brat is still tripped out that I'm the same random girl who booked her for a show in Miami.

Things got off to a rocky start when showtime came around. Biggie hit the stage first and was clearly frustrated by the playback sound quality. It was throwing off his performance. I was backstage, hoping everything would smooth over so the show could go on, but the opposite happened. All of a sudden, the sound engineer was dragged front and center, and punches were flying in a full-on brawl. I was expecting the worst: that the police would get involved and shut the whole show down. All my hard work would have been for nothing. But as quickly as it popped off, security and a couple of the promoters were able to calm everything down. He'd only done about three songs, but that was it for Big's set. Craig Mack was the perfect reset for the audience. The crowd went nuts when he got to "Flava in Ya Ear," even though Biggie didn't return to perform his verse on the remix. His energy seemed to lift everyone's spirits. Brat closed the show out with Jermaine Dupri by her side, and the whole place joined in and sang along to "Funkdafied." Watching the crowds of people leaving after the show was over, talking excitedly about what they'd just seen, and knowing I was partly responsible for making it happen made me so proud of myself. I was still trying not to think about Hollywood, but in that moment, I knew he would have been proud of me, too. If I wanted to, I could have kept throwing events, become a promoter, opened my own spot in Miami and then a chain of clubs all over the South. But I was still trying to silently navigate the throes of grief and was too young to have that kind of foresight.

Hip-hop was moving in closer and intertwining itself into the fabric of my life before I ever laid down a track—from my first Salt-N-Pepa concert to partying on the front lines of the growing Miami bass scene at the Pac Jams, to having a front-row seat to Uncle Luke's solo career and then putting on a full hip-hop concert of my own. There was so much to love about the culture, including the growing connection between hip-hop and fashion, being able to define and set trends. I loved New York swag and really gravitated toward artists like Biggie and Ma$e. When Biggie said, "My Moschino ho, my Versace hottie," I felt like he was talking directly to me and my girls, because we would cop those labels and put our own spin on them. A couple of years later, when Lil' Kim came on the scene as a solo artist, I understood that rap was deeper than the music. It was about a lifestyle, an attitude, and putting the best parts of you on display. Kim's whole vibe was *Move these guys out of the way; the Queen Bitch is here.* She was killing it on her songs, in her outfits, and with her unapologetic personality. She gave sexy and feminine, tough and un-fuck-with-able at the same time. A *woman* was finally making music that my crew and I could relate to and playfully use to define ourselves. We didn't have to pick and choose from the lyrics of men all the time. I was closer in age to Kim, so I felt like I had more in common

with her. She was even short like me. My friend Tika and I listened to Lil' Kim all the time, and one day she looked me dead
in the eye and said, "This is you . . . but Miami." She didn't
have to explain any further, because I knew exactly what she
meant. I was that girl in my city. I wasn't even twenty-one and
I was in music videos, well-connected with the shot-callers,
hitting the hottest spots, and kicking it in clubs with Tupac
and Too $hort on the weekends. Lil' Kim might as well have
been making a soundtrack for my life.

Chapter
8

Trick was released from prison the year after Holly-wood died. He left jail with a bunch of rhymes that he'd already written, and instead of getting any deeper into the street life that had taken his brother from us, Trick dove headfirst into music. As soon as he got out, he immediately linked up with Luke, hoping to sign to his label. But Luke Records was going under because of a lawsuit. Ted was still trying to get Slip-N-Slide Records off the ground, and when Luke filed for bankruptcy, a bunch of former Luke Records employees came to work for him. One of them was Debbie Bennet, who helped teach Ted the business. Trick did a feature on one of Luke's songs—"Scarred"—in 1996, and after it did well, Ted signed Trick to Slip-N-Slide. They were the new big steppers on the city's music scene, and people treated them like kings when they popped out. There was no event or party they couldn't get into, and whenever I was with them, it was full VIP treatment. Trick was still the obnoxious asshole I had always known him to be—maybe even more now that he had so much clout and buzz in the city—but Hollywood's death bonded us together as brother and sister, along with Ted.

My bounce back in the two years since Hollywood passed wasn't looking nearly as promising. I was living with Nessa, helping her take care of my new baby brother. He was named Wilbrent, after his dad, my stepfather, but we all called him Goonkie. Even at three years old, he was the apple of my eye, a bright spot in the darkness of my lingering grief. It was fascinating to watch Nessa in mommy mode with a baby. She was so loving and nurturing. It warmed my heart knowing that she'd probably poured into me the same way when I was little. Laura and I helped as much as we could with changing diapers, making bottles, and keeping our toddler sibling entertained. But after the excitement of the concert wore off, I still needed to figure out what was next for my life.

One of my friends told me about her new job being one of her best financial decisions at a moment when I was desperate to regain control of my life and independence. She told me she danced at a cabaret spot in Fort Lauderdale and brought home hundreds, sometimes thousands, of dollars on a single night. She was doing well for herself, and all her friends could see the changes in her lifestyle and her whole vibe. According to her, they were always looking for new dancers. Talking to Pinkey and one of my cousins about it, I decided to try it out one night only if they promised to do it with me. Emboldened by each other's support, we reasoned that it would be just another one of our crazy nights out. The club was just a topless joint, not fully nude, and it was far enough away from the city that we wouldn't have to worry about running into people we knew. Our friend was seasoned and would show us the ropes.

We packed bags full of stuff we would need for the night: makeup, the tallest heels we had, a sack to hold any money we earned, and outfits, which were actually just bikinis, our skimpiest bra tops, and panties. Then we were on our way. It was still early when we arrived—before midnight—and not even close to crowded. Our friend introduced the three of us to the manager, who looked us up, down, and around. He didn't have any questions for us except how old we were, and then he pointed us to the dressing area. The well-lit room was the total opposite of the dance floor. It smelled like a combination of burnt hair, sweet perfumes, and cigarettes. None of the pretense of seduction or fantasy was necessary back there. As soon as we sat down, the laughter and giggling between the three of us was uncontrollable. What the hell had we gotten ourselves into? We took shots to ease our nerves and started getting ready. We each did quality-assurance checks over our looks, and finally, we were ready to head out onto the floor. I imagined I was walking into any other club I partied at, putting my shoulders back and letting my hips swing a little more as I strutted out in my heels. The club was starting to fill up with customers, and I saw a few guys looking our way almost immediately, just like at a regular party. From those tiny interactions alone, I knew getting guys to pay me for dances wasn't going to be an issue. But what was I going to do after they gave me the money? I knew how to dance to my favorite song at a party or as part of a majorette routine, but neither of those techniques translated into giving a lap dance, climbing the pole, or working the floor at a strip club. Throwing ass is a foundational move in there, and I didn't know how to shake or twerk yet. I strutted around, drawing the gaze of men who clearly wanted some of my attention, but I was looking at what the other dancers were doing. My years of majorette rehearsals and practices came in handy that night because I was still flexible and could easily pick up movements after seeing them a few times.

Pinkey, my cousin, and I stayed within eyesight of each other, and after a few hours, we all had the hang of it. As more people started coming in, I could tell that the three of us were in high demand because we were new. On that first night, I didn't really want to be touched by any of the guys. I didn't hesitate to move out of reach or swat them away if any of them got too handsy. Not sure what to say, I let them lead our conversations. Some of them wanted to know more about me, some of them wanted me to know what kinds of sexual things they would do to me if we were in the bedroom, and some of them wanted to know what I liked in the bedroom. I avoided the questions I didn't want to answer, and most of the guys let me do my dance, tipped me out, and moved on. Every time I took a break in the locker room, I noticed my wad of cash growing. We didn't have to pay the manager on our first night, and when I got home and counted over $3,000 in cash, I knew I was going back. No questions asked.

Honestly, my first few shifts at the club didn't feel like work at all. We were getting paid to shake our asses, drink, and be sexy. I did that for free all the time. These men were drooling and emptying their wallets all night, and we never had to do anything we didn't want to do. There were some similarities, but the strip club was a different environment from dance clubs, with its own set of social norms and rules. Looking good and being confident was only half the battle in there. I made an effort to learn more of the dance moves and bought a few stringy outfits to add to my collection of uniforms. Getting customers to tip more and to pay you to dance for more songs involved a delicate dance of flirtation and finesse. This was a whole new game I had to learn. Some customers were only there for a special occasion or to blow through all the money they'd just come into, not knowing if they'd ever make it back. Those were the ones you drained hard and fast. Some customers weren't as flashy but had careers that allowed them to swing by the club with some regularity. Those were the ones you took your time with, so they'd want to spend money with you during every visit. Having regular customers made you more money, but it was important to pay attention to the relationships being built around you because you didn't want to step on the toes of any of the other dancers. People do not play about their money, and it was *good* money.

I still dreamt of being able to afford my own luxury car and home. I wanted to be able to save and invest my money like I watched Nessa do. I damn sure couldn't do all that making $2,000 a month at AT&T. I justified going back to the club weekend after weekend, month after month, because I wasn't struggling paycheck to paycheck, and I didn't have to sacrifice going out or buying myself nice things. Every night wasn't as lucrative as the first one, but on a couple of occasions I made even more than that. Once I had a taste of how much money I could make in a month at the club, I was hooked. After every weekend, I would say that the next one would be the last, and then another month would pass. To make it worse, I was spending the money almost as fast as I was earning it. I bought myself a car, and I was still going out, which meant I needed new outfits, shoes, and hairdos. So I kept working shifts. What was supposed to be something fun and risky to try one night had turned into my main source of income for almost a year.

Keeping my new job a secret was easy for a while, but word traveled fast. Within a few months, whispers started to reach Nessa that the new booty at the strip club looked a lot like her daughter.

"Is this what you want to do with your life?" The weight of my mom's question hit me like a ton of bricks when she confronted me.

I told her the truth. "No."

Her line of questioning continued. "So, who gave you the idea that this was something cool to do?"

What I wanted her to know, and what *she* really wanted to know, was that I wasn't dancing because I thought it was glamorous or fulfilling. It was a way for me to make decent money until I figured something else out. It was just a stepping stone. To where? I didn't know yet.

"You're being young and reckless right now, but whatever you're doing, figure it out." And that was the end of the discussion.

My mother was right. Unlike the women there who worked at the club to feed their kids and take care of their families, I didn't really need the money. I had a roof over my head and a car that could get me to another job that wouldn't pay as much but would support my future way more than dancing. I was never satisfied with being a pretty face and a nice body, even if I'd reaped the benefits of both. I knew there was more to life. I was raised by women who were smart, ambitious, creative, and respected. Even though I could rock the hell out of a club dress, I saw myself as a boss chick in business suits—a woman who made business deals, not just one who had dollar bills falling all over her body. I knew how to command the power of my sex appeal, but I saw its limitations. I needed to define who I was outside of that. The holidays were approaching, my third year of Christmas cheer without Hollywood, and I started to feel that sense of depression returning. I was empty inside. The attention from the guys at the club wasn't flattering or empowering. I hadn't dated anybody seriously, and the thought of men feeling entitled to touch me annoyed me more than ever before. I'd pull up to the club in a bad mood before the night even started, and the sight of some of my regulars started to disgust me. My purse was always full at the end of a shift, but I dreaded getting ready for the next one. It was time for me to stop or run the risk of getting stuck living a life I hated.

The problem was I didn't know what else I wanted to do. It had been over a year since I had planned the concert, which gave me a goal to work toward and a dream to see through. Low-wage customer-service jobs weren't worth the time they took out of my day. I'd tried a handful of them, and they were boring, they never paid enough, and the ceiling for success at the companies was too low. I didn't want to be a cog in somebody else's machine. Whatever I did next, I wanted it to be significant, I wanted to be proud of it, I wanted to leave my mark on the world. Nessa's words rang louder than ever: *Figure it out*.

Chapter
9

My mom invested her earnings from owning salons into real estate, like the house I moved into after high school. With college and architecture clearly off the table, I wasn't going to design or build properties like my grandfather. However, the business of homes is in my bloodline. What if that was the blueprint I was meant to follow? The more I thought about it, the more being a real estate agent made sense. The earning potential was limitless. I saw myself selling multimillion-dollar homes to the rich and famous of Miami, wearing tailored suits and expensive heels to showings and lunch with clients. I visualized myself as a mogul, hopping out of a brand-new Porsche with a perfect slicked-back ponytail. Even though I was still working shifts at the strip club, I finally knew what my next move would be. I was going to get my real estate license.

One of the biggest selling points of my plan was that I could start the process of getting certified immediately. At that time, all you had to do was pass the real estate certification exam and then the state board test to be qualified to work as an agent in Florida. I had two options to prepare for the tests: a two-month prep class or a weeklong cram course. They both cost a few hundred bucks, but it was a no-brainer which one I was going to take. My mind was made up, and I felt that fire under my ass to make something happen. I had to strike while the iron was hot. While I was in the cram class, I turned my beeper off, I didn't take any calls, I didn't go hang out, and I only worked on the weekend. Then I dedicated another two weeks to studying. I felt like I was on a secret mission. I only told my mom, my sister, Pinkey, and Angie what I was doing holed up in my room. I studied and practiced for that final exam harder than I'd ever done for a test in school.

On the day of the exam, I walked into the small room with a group of people from different racial backgrounds and generations. I was definitely one of the youngest people there. I grabbed my seat, waited for the test to start, and put all those hours of preparation to work. It only took a few days to find out, via automated phone call, that I'd passed on the first try. Nessa beamed from ear to ear and gave me the biggest hug when I told her. I think both of us were relieved that I was picking myself up out of my despair and making progress in life. I had to schedule a date for my state board exam next. There were a few weeks between the two exams, so I went back to work at the club in the meantime, but I made a promise to myself that if I got certified to do real estate, I was quitting. I was actually able to enjoy those last few weeks because I knew my time was coming to an end. I tried to make as much money as I could before I was out for good. The state board test was longer and more intense than the certification exam. I wasn't nearly as sure about my performance when it was done. I said a silent prayer that everything would work out. In the few weeks it took to receive my results in the mail, I started to doubt myself. But I had no reason to: I passed my state boards. I never went back to the club.

I finalized my application to become a registered real estate agent and received my license in the mail. From start to finish, the entire process took me about three months, but I was ready to start building my empire immediately. I applied for jobs at several real estate agencies to get my foot in the door. I was offered an entry-level position at a brokerage called E. R. Homeland Realty, which meant I'd be supporting other more established agents until I had clients and listings of my own. My first month was spent handling administrative tasks like printing and organizing listings, making phone calls to potential buyers and sellers, and sitting in on meetings to learn the ropes.

My colleagues respected my hustle and eagerness, and when a young family expressed interest in one of the properties we represented, they trusted me to take care of them. I was so excited. I read and reread the listing details so I'd know everything about the house. On the day of the showing, I put extra effort into my outfit. I wanted the clients to respect that

I was professional and put together. My dress was formfitting but not too tight, and my heels were cute but sensible. I'd recently had a fresh Dominican blowout, so my hair was silky and bouncy. I swept my lids with a little bit of eyeshadow and applied a fresh coat of lip gloss before I left. The couple showed up with their baby, excited to add buying a house to their list of firsts together. It was the first place they were looking at together as a family. As we walked through the house, I guided them through the experience as if they already lived there, calling out the best features and how they might use them in their everyday life. They didn't have many questions, but the ones they did have I was on top of. They loved the house, and I just knew I killed it. There was a good possibility that I was about to earn my first commission as a real estate agent. I wasn't standing on a stepping stone anymore; I was on my path. But I was about to hit a fork in the road.

Chapter
10

By the time I got my real estate license, Trick's first album, *Based on a True Story*, was out and charting on Billboard. Slip-N-Slide was on the map, and I was so happy to see Ted's vision thriving. They'd accepted the torch passed by Luke, using the music industry to represent Miami. Still, when Trick initially asked me to come to the studio and jump on a record he was working on, I said no. I wasn't trying to be a rapper and was sure he could find somebody else to do it. I brushed him off, hoping he wouldn't bring it up again. But in true Trick fashion, he persisted. *It ain't that serious, Trina. I just need you to talk some shit on this record!* I could never catch a break with him.

The night I went to the studio to record just so happened to be the same day that I finally did my first showing as a real estate agent. I was still riding that high and daydreaming about the future of my career when I rolled up to the small home studio. Pinkey, Angie, and our other two friends, Tika and Michelle, met me there. Slip-N-Slide's in-house producer, Funk Boogie, was waiting for us. It was a tiny room with a couch, a chair, and some mixing equipment stuffed in, and the booth was pretty much a closet with a mic and some soundproofing. It was exactly the kind of "creative" atmosphere you would expect from local rappers. It's funny how guys who walk around with thousands of dollars in their pockets can spend so much time in a janky spot to make their music. But that's how it was with street guys. They made money in rough places—like projects or raggedy studios—so that they could afford all the nice vibes later.

The song was called "Nann," and Trick had already laid his verse and the hook, and Funk invited me to step into the booth to hear it. My friends and I locked eyes in disbelief as it blasted through the speakers and the words sank in. All of us were used to dating aggressive street guys, and we grew up on 2 Live Crew. The lyrics weren't shocking because they were vulgar. Trick was prone to saying off-the-wall stuff all the time, and his music was always hard-core, so that wasn't surprising, either. It was the duality of him addressing a woman he wants to get with but spitting all of his raw street shit in the process. The song was already filled with so much audacity. What the hell did Trick want me to do with it?! Funk saw me struggling with what to do next and suggested I just lay down my version of the hook, which said, "You don't know nann ho" instead of "nann nigga." It took a couple of takes for me to get comfortable and perfect my delivery. We recorded a few layers, and by the time we were done, Trick walked in with a couple of other guys from the label.

We had a good laugh sharing our honest first reactions to "Nann" with him. That's when he explained that he needed me to talk my shit on a verse but from a female perspective. For the first time, I understood my assignment. "Nann" was a combative battle-of-the-sexes type of song that could appeal to a wider audience because it offered different perspectives. It was cocky, in-your-face, bold as hell but somehow still flirty. (That might seem like a contradiction, but it's an approach that Florida guys have down pat.) Trick's lyrics were a challenge, and after I heard his verse, I used the same approach I did when guys like him tried to holla at me on the street: *Whatever you do, I can do better.*

Funk played the track from the top again, and I used Trick's verse as a road map, listening line by line to think of rebuttals to his bars. If he could spend money, so could I. If he was nasty, so was I. If he could "run through [my] whole lil' crew," then I could "fuck 'bout five or six best friends." Pinkey, Angie, Tika, and Michelle made sure their pagers were off, and they found open seats on the couch and the floor to wait quietly while I rapped into the mic. Between recordings, I bounced ideas off of them. To be clear, a lot of what I said on "Nann" are things I would *never* do in real life—at least not *all* of them—but we playfully let ourselves imagine some of the most foul-mouthed rebuttals. I put so much heart into it because I was having a good time. I felt like I had something to prove, and my girls were right there, gassing me up. You'd never know from my sharp, serious tone how much I laughed through my "Nann" verse.

It was two in the morning by the time my verse was finally arranged, recorded with the ad-libs, and layered as Funk saw fit. I couldn't lie—I was hella impressed with the final product. Trick and the guys were in love with the song and amped up on a hundred as we played it back. They were bouncing around and bopping their heads and singing the words loudly. All my girls rapped over my verse. Trick was so geeked by my verse he kept yelling, "Trina, you the baddest bitch out here!" He called Ted and convinced him to get out of bed and come listen to the finished song. Hearing my part, Ted looked at me with these wide eyes and then started hooting and hollering with everybody else. There was no denying that "Nann" was a hit, and even though I had a blast making it, I saw it as a win for Slip-N-Slide, not me.

The next day I went to get a pedicure from my friend B. He was a gay guy and the only person I trusted with my nails. I liked going to see him later in the evening as his last appointment so that we could catch up alone. We had deep, satisfying conversations about everything as he worked on my toes, and this day was no different. "I gotta tell you what I did," I blurted out as soon as I was in the chair.

"Bitch, what?!" He could tell by my tone I had some real tea to spill, and he couldn't wait to sip it.

When I told him that I'd recorded a whole verse on one of Trick Daddy's songs, he couldn't believe it. He knew that I hung out with rappers, but he didn't think I'd ever be one. I felt comfortable playing the tape so he could hear the song. When he heard my verse, he went crazy just like Trick, Ted, and the rest of the guys in the studio had. "The girls are going to live for it, and the gays are going to eat it up!" The excitement was just running through his body. He told me I should think about rapping more often and follow the success of "Nann" wherever it took me. He wouldn't let me accept that this was a one-time experience I could just forget about. He was the first person outside of the industry to think I was onto something big.

"I can't do that. People are going to think I'm a freak! I'm trying to get into real estate!" The way I looked at it, the music industry was part of my social life, not my professional one. Just like partying and doing ratchet shit with my friends, hanging around rappers, and dropping explicit verses was something I did for fun. That's who I was when I wasn't pursuing my *real* dreams. But my friend / nail tech would not take that as an answer. He saw something in my future I wasn't ready to accept. I left his shop still afraid of what my mother would say if she heard it, how my family would react, and how my new real estate colleagues might look at me. There was a tiny part of me that saw exactly what my friend saw—a banger that the girls (and the gays) were going to love. But what did that have to do with me?

"Nann" was released in 1998. The club DJs put it in rotation immediately, and it generated buzz all over the South. It was hard to get radio play because the lyrics weren't kid friendly, but an edited version was on its way. It was the last song Trick recorded for his second album and the obvious lead single, so Ted started working to get national radio play and shop the album around to major labels. As soon as it came out, "Nann" was the only song you heard in Miami. It was playing at the block parties, in car stereos, at the football games, and at the bars. You couldn't escape it. Only a few people knew that I was the female voice on the track, so I got to enjoy the fanfare in relative peace for a while.

Trick had a show booked in the city a couple of weeks later, and I rolled with him to support. The bottles were popping in VIP. All the fly girls were out and dressed to the nines. There were real moneymakers and hustlers in the building letting themselves have a good time for a few hours. I watched Trick do his thing from backstage and saw the crowd get hyped as soon as they heard the bass drop at the beginning of "Nann." The transition interlude, where I'm flat out rejecting him, came on and I felt someone pushing me onstage. I didn't know who it was; I just heard them yelling at me, "Go! Go! Gooo!"

I frantically tried to resist being put on the stage, but I was in view of the audience, with a mic forced into my hand, before I could do anything. There were at least a few hundred people staring at me, already hyped. My verse started, and I couldn't bring myself to rap the words in public. I was absolutely frozen with fear.

"You don't know nann ho
Done been the places I been
Who could spend the grands that I spend . . ."

I closed my eyes and silently prayed that the moment would be over. I stood completely still, not uttering a word. But a chorus of women's voices were singing at the top of their lungs in unison:

"Fuck 'bout five or six best friends
You don't know nann ho"

They recited the whole verse, word for word, with pride. Every bar got them more geeked as they went along.

Meanwhile, the thought of rapping about giving head and selling tail so explicitly made me bashful. I had assumed that was true for other girls, too, but I was wrong. They felt no shame. As soon as my part was over, I damn near ran off the stage. I'm pretty sure I cursed out the first person I saw from Trick's team. How dare they set me up like that. But hearing the crowd's reaction to my verse definitely shifted my mindset. There was obviously *something* about the raunchiness that women were identifying with. These women—women from *my* city—were clearly hungry for music and artists that represented *that* part of them. They wanted an anthem that was freaky and uninhibited, too. That's what artists like Trick Daddy, Uncle Luke, and pretty much every other male rapper offered men. That night at the show, I realized I could give that gift to women.

I've exuded bad-bitch energy since I was a teenager. That's why Trick knew to call me, out of all the girls he knew, to lay the verse. With this one part of a song, I could transfer that energy and give other ladies permission to channel it for themselves.

Within a week of that performance, Ted gently suggested that I sign with Slip-N-Slide and make an album of my own. As far as I was concerned, he was out of his mind for even considering something like that. Nessa didn't even know that I'd done the verse, and I dreaded her response to me talking crazy. There was no way I was going to make a career out of it, and I told Ted as much. But I couldn't use that excuse for very long.

"What is wrong with your mouth?!" Nessa demanded to know. The question wasn't rhetorical.

Before I told on myself, I asked her what she was talking about. She had finally heard "Nann." Thankfully, it was the edited radio version, but my mother wasn't a fool. She could easily read between the lines. I tried to downplay the whole situation like it was just an inside joke that went too far among my friends. I did my best to convince her that I would never in a million years repeat those things, or write more songs like it, or perform in front of thousands of people. She rolled her eyes and accepted that answer. Nessa didn't know that Ted was actively trying to get me to sign a record deal where I would get paid to do all the things I told her I had no intention of doing. She also didn't know what it felt like hearing all those women react to my verse the first time I was onstage when it played.

As "Nann" kept growing, the hard work Ted was putting into promotion for Trick's album was paying off. The buzz generated from the song helped land Slip-N-Slide a major distribution deal with Atlantic that put them on the national stage. Ted wasn't taking my no for an answer about signing with the label. Trick was booking more and more shows, and the team at the label wanted me to try hitting the stage again. He was scheduled to perform in Tallahassee at Florida A&M University's homecoming. Feeling a little more confident and prepared, I agreed. I had time to pick an outfit and have my mom do my hair. I even worked with backup dancers to liven up the stage. We were booked at a club called the Moon, and it was a way bigger crowd than the club where I froze up.

As soon as the beat dropped for "Nann," the place went wild. I kept my eyes open and said all the words this time. I fed off the crowd's energy. Once footage from that performance got back to the label, Ted upped the pressure to get me to sign with Slip-N-Slide. He knew I had something to offer the music industry, but now Atlantic Records did, too. Reps from both teams called me multiple times, asking me to reconsider a record deal. Ted demanded that I come meet with him in his office as soon as we got back to the city. With the Atlantic deal in place and the song gaining nationwide traction, the circumstances were different. I could no longer brush Slip-N-Slide off, because everyone on the label was my friend. They were backed by a major label now, with international reach.

In the days leading up to the meeting with Ted, I thought seriously about my future. I still wanted to be successful off the strength of my own hard work and name. I'd dedicated so much time and effort to get my real estate license, but I had a long road ahead until I reached true financial independence with it. Back then, the music industry wasn't nearly as saturated as it is today. If you knew the right people, blew up in your city, and got the right opportunity, you could make some life-changing bread. The deal Ted was offering would definitely give me a good head start. When I looked at it from this perspective, I saw that I wasn't being pulled away from my dreams; I was being offered an alternative route to get there. I couldn't deny the love and excitement that fans had for "Nann," and I knew we had enough momentum to make it work. The icing on the cake was that I wasn't putting my future in the hands of some stranger who rode in on a dark horse, promising me the world. Ted and Trick were like family to me, and I trusted them. I invited Ted over to Nessa's before the meeting because I'd made up my mind.

By the time I signed my record deal with Slip-N-Slide, the offense Nessa took to my "Nann" verse had worn off. Even she had to admit the song was catchy. Plus, she and Ted had a good face-to-face conversation about how this deal would affect me. I didn't know anything about the music industry, and my mom was aware of my naïveté, but she trusted Ted had my back. Like me, she was also reassured by Slip-N-Slide's new ties to Atlantic as a professional, reputable company. Putting my name on that dotted line came with a $250,000 advance. It was the most money I had ever received at one time. Just a year earlier, I was dancing at a strip club, hoping to make $10,000 a month; now I was looking at six figures after a few hours of work on one song. It was surreal. We had a celebra-tory dinner, and I handed the check right over to Nessa. She put part of it away for savings and used another portion to invest and help me build a safety net. I'm forever grateful I had her in my corner.

Chapter
11

Making the music video for "Nann" was the first time I really got to see the full force of a record label at work. Slip-N-Slide's rep at Atlantic was a guy named Mike Caren, who was still an intern. He sat us down for a meeting with their creative team where they went over the different treatments and concepts for the video. Most of it was shot at the Tropigala Lounge, a club in the Fontainebleau hotel, for a party scene. I invited a bunch of my homegirls, including Pinkey, Tika, Michelle, and Angie, to be in the video. I spent hours in glam getting my makeup done while assistants made sure all the outfits were pressed to perfection and ready to go. The label didn't spare a dime, but I still had Nessa do my hair. (For the first year of my career, she was still the only person I trusted to get my hair right.) There were so many celebrities who came out to party with us and have cameos in "Nann," like Chico DeBarge, JT Money, Luke, and a bunch of Miami athletes.

The hardest part of filming was pretending to take Trick seriously. I was struggling not to laugh every time we had to do a scene together because it felt so ridiculous. I know the director was probably annoyed at how many takes we had to do of those scenes because I couldn't keep it together.

When the video was released, I had to wait to see it until it came on MTV, BET, or The Box like everyone else. But it was worth the wait because the video was so dope. Seeing myself on TV as a main character was wild. I always knew I was sexy, but after getting the professional glam experience, I was a different *kind* of sexy. I looked like a real celebrity. I had never seen my own curves from some of those angles, and I didn't realize that slow motion could make me look so seductive. For the first time, I thought I actually looked as glamorous as Sheila E. in "The Glamorous Life."

With the single and video in rotation to support Trick's album, it was time to hit the road. We had shows booked pretty much every weekend. After the main performance, we would do walk-throughs and maybe a mini set at different clubs. Once again, I was getting paid to be sexy, party, and put on a show, but unlike at the strip club, I was keeping my clothes on and doing it all over the United States. I was paid around $5,000 for each show, minus expenses and the cut set aside for my team. Over a single weekend, I made more than I did in a good month working at the club.

Slip-N-Slide hired Redd as my road manager. He was

savvy and already close to the team and me. He kept everything organized and got shit done while I was on the road. For every concert, radio station appearance, and photoshoot, Redd was the one making sure everything went smoothly. He took care of hotels and travel arrangements, confirmed the money was good before we stepped onstage, and made sure I had everything I needed while I was on the road. He also helped manage me and my emotions when shit got rough. Our workdays were long, sometimes starting at 7 a.m. to make a morning radio show and not ending until two or three the next morning, when a show's after-party was done. When we did get sleep, it was usually in a cramped, moving bus or sometimes on a plane. Whenever I had meltdowns because I felt like I messed up onstage, something went wrong with my wardrobe or choreography, or our logistics were thrown off, Redd was the calming presence I needed. Trick and his guys, on the other hand, could be super chaotic. They didn't miss a single opportunity to party and turn up. Women were always around, willing to do whatever they could to get Trick's attention. It was normal to catch glimpses of asses and titties at all hours of the night in our hotels. It was wild being the only woman traveling with a group of men. All of it was worth it, though, because after only really traveling to places in the South, the Caribbean, and New York, I finally got to see the rest of the country.

I went from dreading that first performance with Trick to falling in love with being onstage. I learned to pay attention to body language and crowd participation. Each audience was like a person with their own unique characteristics. Depending on the location, the demographic, and the size of the crowd, I would get different energy, and I had to work with what was in front of me. Some crowds would be so hyped that I would let them recite my entire "Nann" verse first, then have the DJ run the beat back so that I could do it. For crowds that were more male dominated, I turned up the sex appeal and made sure I danced seductively. A little call-and-response could always wake up a dead audience.

During that first year on the road, I never traveled without my headphones and a notebook. Atlantic was putting all hands on deck to promote Trick's single, but behind the scenes, they were zoned in on me. I signed my deal in 1999, and they gave me a hard deadline of one year to get my debut album completed. They were already starting to develop me as an artist. I was in a situation that so many other aspiring rappers dreamt about: backed by a major label that wanted to see me succeed. I had skipped the line, which was both a blessing and a curse. Because I hadn't put in the same amount of work that a lot of my peers did, I had to learn to develop my craft from the ground up. I didn't know anything about songwriting or music production and had a lot of catching up to do to meet the standards that were expected of me. I basically had to learn how to be a recording artist because this was my job now.

Chapter

12

Most of the beats Slip-N-Slide sent me for my first album were made by C.O. (who was one half of Tre+6, the first duo signed to the label) and Deuce Poppi. I listened to them when we traveled between cities, and when I liked one, I started jotting down ideas and notes that would serve as the foundation of the song. After being on the road from Thursday through Sunday, I'd touch back down in Miami and either hit the studio right away to record or spend hours writing. I remember sitting outside Nessa's house in my car, listening to beats and trying to tweak certain lyrics to make a song more catchy or interesting. I put a lot of pressure on myself to make songs I thought women would like and flock to, even if they were just as gritty and street as the songs Trick had. I pulled inspiration from things I'd seen or been through in Miami, sometimes calling my homegirls to listen to what they were going through in their personal lives and writing about that.

But my environment on tour wasn't lacking in source material, either. I paid attention to how the women who came to our concerts dressed, how they spoke, and how they acted at the clubs and backstage. I listened to their stories as moms, students, girlfriends, dancers, and hustlers. Even the girls that Trick and his crew brought back to the hotel or tour bus gave me good material to draw from. I tried to put myself in their shoes and then take it to the next level. I played my own little mental game of What Would the Baddest Bitch Do? What would I do if I met someone that I was a fan of, like LL Cool J, and was trying to get him in bed? How would I make myself stand out in a crowd of women who all wanted the same thing so that I was the one taking him down in the back of the tour bus? If a guy wanted to date me, how would I go about making him prove himself? I didn't want to sound preachy or judgmental in my music; I wanted female listeners to feel like they were getting realness and learning the game. My mission was to get women to level up and tap into their bad-bitch energy.

I showed up to that first studio session with my notebook of rhymes feeling like most of the work was done, which couldn't have been further from the truth. There are so many small details that go into making just one song, from the lyrics to the beat, to the features, to the vocals. I was on a steep learning curve and still figuring out the strategy for it all. One of my main struggles was my voice. When I first started rapping, I hated how squeaky my voice sounded and would try to change it in the booth by making it deeper. Attempting to give my voice bass that it didn't have was too straining, and I couldn't maintain it through a whole song. My team always loved the way I sounded, though, because it was surprisingly different from my lyrical content. It's what gave me a distinct trademark, and they pushed me to embrace it, so I did.

One of the things that surprised me in the beginning was how much starting and stopping it took to get a song done. I thought once it was written, I could just go in and record the whole song straight through as long as I didn't mess up. C.O. and Rick Ross, who was another Miami artist building out his rap career and producing, would stop me mid-verse to adjust how I delivered certain bars, or pull a line from the verse that they thought would be better for the hook and rearrange the whole thing. They had an ear for production, always knowing when to layer vocals or punch the beat out. Once I understood the mechanics of song composition, I started to obsess over those details, too. Even when we weren't in the studio together, I was calling them to get their input. This really was like a training camp on how to make music.

Even though I was a new artist, my team let me dream big for my first album. Some of the first songs we did, like "Off Glass" and "Pull Over," had a similar vibe to "Nann." They were raw and raunchy, but if this album was really going to be a reflection of me, it had to include all the different pieces of my personality. I wasn't just a slick-mouth moneymaker. I had a sensitive, soft side that I also wanted to express by playing with different sounds.

Total is one of the R & B girl groups of the '90s I was obsessed with. Their voices were so silky when they harmonized, and I listened to their self-titled debut album and the follow-up, *Kima, Keisha & Pam*, all the time. As soon as I got the green light for my project, I knew I wanted them on it. Redd started making calls to their management team. There was a little bit of back-and-forth, and in the end, I didn't get the Total feature I wanted. I had Pam and Keisha on two different songs instead. That was still a win for me. The rest of the features on that album came to be based on what I thought the vibe should be. When I heard the quick bounce in the beat for "Watch Yo Back," the first person I thought to have on the track with me was Twista. He was known for rapping faster and sharper than anybody else out at the time, so I knew he could keep up with the track and make it memorable. No one argued with me when I insisted that I have a song dedicated to my mama, even though it didn't fit into the overall theme of the album. Instead, the team found a slow, melodic beat to set a sentimental mood, got J-Shin to sing the hook, and let me lay the verses down.

There was never any question about what the title of my first album would be. Trick had spoken the words out loud on the night I recorded "Nann," and they stuck. Sometimes he still used it to introduce me onstage for performances. Even Ted agreed that it just made sense for my official music debut. I had gotten everyone's attention on "Nann" by being bold, sexy, and unapologetic. I was doubling down on that with the songs I had been writing. Everybody wanted to know what the short girl with the slick mouth and the big booty was about. It was time for me to introduce myself, and at my core, I was "da baddest bitch."

We thought the album name was so strong that it didn't need a title track. My first single, "Da Baddest Bitch," was actually one of the last songs we made for the album. But when we heard the beat for that record, which originally included a sample of Michael Jackson's song "Bad," we knew we had struck gold. The low horns made it feel taunting and commanding. It needed to deliver all the raw sexuality, all the shit talk, and all the unapologetic energy that my growing fan base wanted. I took a few days writing and reworking the verses until I felt like it was perfect. We made Trick rush to the studio and rerecord the "Who's bad?!" line as a background ad-lib so we wouldn't get hit with a copyright suit from Michael Jackson. When we played the final version back in the studio, the energy was celebratory and infectious just like when we wrapped "Nann." We didn't know it at the time, but we had just made another hip-hop classic.

For a long time, the music video for "Da Baddest Bitch" was the most expensive one Slip-N-Slide had ever done, costing a little over a million dollars. I played a woman who was so pissed when she found out her man was cheating that she destroyed all his belongings. It was a simple premise, but it was costly because I literally had to break furniture and jewelry and push a car into the water. I had a ball taking a bat to glass tables and vases without having to worry about the consequences. Warren Sapp was a defensive tackle for the Tampa

Bay Buccaneers and one of the best players in the NFL. Before he went pro, he played for the University of Miami and got to know Trick on the music scene. He was one of the city's big ballers, so him playing the role of my cheating man was bound to generate even more buzz.

When it was time to preview the album for Mike's bosses at Atlantic, I was nervous. Even though they signed me because I was bringing Southern flavor to raunchy female rap, it still felt weird to play the songs in front of a group of professionals in a meeting room. They started jamming to it once we were a few tracks in, and my nerves faded away. They loved it. I delivered everything they wanted. It was the fuel for the girls, with some street vibes for the guys. It gave grunge; it gave fly girl. It gave raw, sexy, raunchy. *Da Baddest Bitch* gave everything that Miami represents. The Atlantic marketing team got their wheels spinning right away on how to creatively package the project. We all agreed that the images needed to exude power, and that's exactly what they did.

I made sure I had a lot of say in the styling and looks for the shoot. Nessa only worked with my natural hair for the entire spread of images, which would be unheard of today in an industry where so many editorial and cover looks are achieved with wigs and weaves. We kept it down for some of the glamour shots, she put it in a ponytail to tuck under a nurse hat for the scene that made the cover, and she gave me a pinup for the look where I got to rock a suit. The latter was my favorite, and not just because of the hair. I was sitting on top of a desk in a skirt suit and strappy heels, with my legs crossed, looking like the head of a Fortune 500 corporation. We hired a male model from an agency to kneel in front of me as a footrest. There I was, a powerful woman in a suit, just like I thought I would be when I finally stepped into my purpose. It was a full-circle, self-actualized vision. The pictures of me staring directly into the camera oozing glitz and seduction are amazing, but that shot was special.

I have to give credit to the Atlantic marketing team for that final iconic cover shot where I'm a sexy paramedic strad-dling an injured man outside of an ambulance. It looks like I have the power over whether he lives or dies because I have the defibrillator paddles to his chest. But instead of looking down at him, I'm staring dead into the camera, licking my lips with sultry eyes. One of the creatives who pitched it gave the rationale that after *Da Baddest Bitch* dropped, any man who heard it or even met a chick who listened to it would need a lifesaver, because I was *killing* them. Hence, the patient on the gurney fighting for his life. The cover also worked as a play on the idea that I was breathing new life into hip-hop. Fans have also taken different meanings from it: Men who fanta-size about being between the legs of a sexy woman see it as an invitation to take the patient's place on the stretcher, an-ticipating a satisfying outcome for themselves. Women who know the power of feminine sexuality toy with the idea that I'm the reason he required a stretcher in the first place, which can be sexy in its own way. The fact that it's spurred so much speculation is the beauty of it.

My first album hit record store shelves in March 2000.

I didn't have a traditional release party, because I was doing promo in different cities up to the day of the drop. We hit BET in Washington, DC, and ended up in New York the day it came out to do MTV. We had to work super hard to push "Da Baddest Bitch" because it was so provocative—even the edited version—that it didn't get as much radio play as we wanted. It charted on Billboard's Hot R&B/Hip-Hop Songs at no. 64. The next single, "Pull Over," did better. It charted on the Hot 100, Hot R&B/Hip-Hop, and Hot Rap Songs. My album debuted on the Billboard 200 and stayed there for thirty-nine weeks. It was on the Top R&B/Hip-Hop Albums chart for forty-nine weeks. The streets were buzzing about the project because it was so explicit and in-your-face, but it also wasn't set to the kinds of beats that people were used to hearing in the industry. That made people take notice of what I was bringing to the game.

Ludacris and I met when we were booked for the same show in one of the cities on my whirlwind first year of touring. He was a radio DJ turned independent artist who was performing songs from his first album. One of them was "What's Your Fantasy?," which featured a verse by Shawnna, a female rapper from Chicago. The song had the South in a choke hold, and he got in touch with my team about being on the remix. This was one of my first features outside the Slip-N-Slide family, so I took a few days to write the verse, wanting to give it my all. I made sure it still had bossed-up energy and added something new to the song. I loved the way it came out, but I was blown away when I found out

Foxy Brown was on it, too. She was a beast on the mic and killed the track. Putting two more women on the remix took "What's Your Fantasy?" to a completely different level, and Luda's fans ate it right up. Even when I wasn't billed with Ludacris, I added that verse to my set list because I knew the crowd would enjoy it.

.... ✦ ....

What the public didn't know during those first two years on the road was that I was in a relationship the entire time. He's an extremely private person and still very important to me, so out of respect, I won't name him. But he played a huge role in my healing from the grief of losing Hollywood and adjusting to my new career in the spotlight. During the promo tour for *Da Baddest Bitch*, I was feeling sick and more tired than I usually did on the road. I bought an at-home pregnancy test, and when the results confirmed I was pregnant, I was overcome with a mixture of emotions. At that age, I still looked forward to the day I might become a mother myself. I was watching my little brother grow up, and I loved him more and more each day. I admired Nessa and the way she took care of her family. I wanted to be that for someone else.

A kid of my own was something I hoped to have in my future, not my present, though. It was the wrong time. Slip-N-Slide had invested so much into my career and my album. There was a lot of money riding on me being able to show up and show out as "da baddest bitch." Pregnancy is a beautiful thing, but it wasn't going to help the brand I had just started building. My career was going in the direction everyone wanted it to go. Plans for a follow-up album, additional tour dates, and a bunch of promotional appearances were already in the works. A baby was about to bring all of it to a halt. I cried when I delivered the news to Nessa, who tried to convince me that a baby didn't have to mean the end of my life.

Resigned to the fact that my career was going to fold in a few months, I tried to look forward to my life as a mother. In the meantime, I committed to making the most of what time I had left. I chose to keep the pregnancy a secret from the public and my label for as long as I could. Forging ahead, I kept up with all my scheduled appearances and shows for the next few weeks. I was able to stop drinking without anyone noticing, and I tried to limit how much smoke I was exposed to. One morning, I woke up on the tour bus and noticed I was spotting, and I didn't feel right. I dreaded going to the emergency room, because I didn't need them to tell me what I already knew. But I went, and they delivered the news I was expecting: I was losing the baby.

As quickly as I had gotten my hopes up about becoming a mom, they came crashing down once I miscarried. It was a quick sadness, like having an ice-cold bucket of water thrown on you from the inside out. It numbed me, but not in any way that brought relief. There was no bottom to the emptiness I felt, and it made me grateful to have so much to distract myself with. There was no time to dwell on that sadness, especially when not many people knew what was going on with me in the first place. I stayed busy to keep the overwhelming disappointment away. I threw myself into my career and took my miscarriage as a sign that the timing just wasn't right.

I would have been a fool to slow down at that point. I said yes to every red carpet, every event, and every party. My man and I probably should have used our alone time to process what had happened, but I was still a twentysomething, suddenly afraid that the world would pass me by while I was sitting at home. Up until that point, I liked that my man brought so much order and organization to my life. I didn't mind that he, a classic Aquarius, liked to keep his partying to a minimum and stay behind the scenes. He was my calm in the storm of a hectic industry. Meanwhile, my Sagittarius was on full display. The promise of the next adventure was the only thing that kept my attention. After *Da Baddest Bitch* dropped, Trick and I had the city in a frenzy. His third album, *Book of Thugs: Chapter A.K., Verse 47*, came out a month before mine, so we both had music in circulation, getting radio play. We were the only artists from Miami getting that level of national notoriety at the time. The level of access and respect we had in the city was unmatched. We pulled up with groups of twenty to thirty people at every spot we hit, and the venue always made room to accommodate us without question. Any event with our names on it was the one everyone wanted to be at because we brought out all the baddest bitches, all the ballers, and all the celebrities. We shut shit down every time. I was in my prime. If there were any questions about Trina being the baddest bitch of Miami, I laid them to rest after my album dropped. The limelight felt like a remedy for the discomfort I felt in a body that betrayed me.

It was hard to articulate how complicated my feelings were, so I just didn't. Instead, I went out for days at a time without coming home when we were in Miami. My man was more patient than I ever would have been in the same situation, calling and pleading with me to come home so we could talk about our issues like adults. I'd give him an excuse for why I couldn't. When I'd finally make it home, I'd try to dodge the issue some more. No relationship can survive when the lines of communication are severed, and a few months after I lost the baby, we had to accept that our romantic relationship was at the end of its rope. He was ready to show me what a life of peace could look like, but in 2001, I wasn't ready to settle down, and I didn't want to see it.

Chapter
13

This might come as a surprise, because the entertainment industry has a reputation for being isolating, but my first two years as an artist brought some beautiful connections to fruition. In Miami, people knew me before I signed a deal, so I didn't think I was being treated any differently at home. My cousin Joy worked at the swap meet, which was always popping on the weekends. It was to hood Miami people what a mall was to white teenagers in the suburbs. You could get your hair braided and buy a knockoff Gucci bag all in the same place. One of the shops at the swap had pictures of me posted to promote their services. Joy's co-worker Camari saw it, and when he found out we were related, he wanted to know if my Dominican blowout was all my real hair. It became an ongoing point of conversation between them, and when I was finally at the swap to see Joy, she insisted that we be introduced. I playfully confronted him. "Why you so worried about my hair? Yes, it's real!"

Camari tried to act nonchalant, like he wasn't pressed, and it became a running joke that he "knew I had a weave" every time I saw him. A few months after that first interaction, the "Nann" video was released. Joy let me know that when Camari saw his new friend with the pretty hair in it, he *freaked* out. But when I saw him again, he was back to his normal sassy self, acting like he wasn't impressed at all. I loved his genuine good energy, and that was the beginning of another endearing friendship that's still going today.

Part of the press leading up to *Da Baddest Bitch* was a *Vibe* magazine feature about the rise of female rappers. I did a group photoshoot with Rah Digga, Solé, Mocha, Charli Baltimore, and Eve, the first lady of Ruff Ryders from Philly. Eve was so gorgeous that she could effortlessly rock a blonde fade, but she rode motorcycles, handled pit bulls, and mean mugged with East Coast realness. We were drawn to each other on set and chatted casually in our downtime. We had a lot in common. Our careers were taking off at the same time, we'd both danced at strip clubs, and we were both trying to adjust to our new normal. We were young women in an extremely competitive field where support and advice aren't always readily available. I didn't know how badly I needed the camaraderie of another woman who understood what I was going through as a new artist until I met her. We exchanged numbers so we could stay in touch after the shoot and were always texting or calling each other. Eve became my first friend in the industry. We made it a point to link up when we were in the same city: New York. LA. Miami. We let loose on both coasts and in between.

Watching Eve's success was such an inspiration for me. Her first album, *Let There Be Eve . . . Ruff Ryders' First Lady*, debuted at no. 1 on the Billboard 200 in 1999. A few years later, she proved her crossover appeal when she collaborated with Gwen Stefani on "Let Me Blow Ya Mind." That song got Eve her first Grammy. She made me feel like there were no limits on what I could accomplish as an artist.

In 2000, I was getting ready to perform for BET's annual Spring Bling, a televised weekend of live hip-hop and R & B music for Black spring breakers in Daytona Beach. My stomach flew into a fit of butterflies when I got a call from Mona Scott-Young. She was a power player in the industry after she cofounded the game-changing hip-hop label and management company, Violator. Her company was responsible for taking the careers of superstars like A Tribe Called Quest and Busta Rhymes to new heights with innovate partnerships and brand deals. She said, "Someone wants to meet you." That someone was her artist, Missy Elliott. I was shook. Missy was already a legend. She could rap. She could sing. She could dance. She could come up with some of the most mind-blowing visuals. She could produce the records. She wrote some of my favorite

Aaliyah and Total songs, and her album *Supa Dupa Fly* stayed in my rotation. Everything Missy touched was fire. I knew she was going to be at Spring Bling with her new artist, Tweet, but I couldn't believe she wanted to meet me.

I made sure my team carved out time for us to connect, and we made plans for me to go to her trailer. I was a ball of giddy nerves leading up to it. She was in glam, getting ready for her set, when I got there. She opened her arms wide to pull me in for a big hug. Then she made a joke about wanting to meet the woman who had been "talking so much shit" in her songs. She'd heard my music. I could have melted on the spot.

Later that day, I watched Tweet and Missy give amazing performances, still smiling to myself about the meeting. On TV, Spring Bling looked like a music festival, with a bunch of performances and interviews happening on a beach. Experiencing it in person was completely different. It was a huge party weekend in Daytona in a time before social media. As artists, we would turn up on the beach during the day and hit the clubs at night. Missy invited me to come hang at the party she was going to that night, and I didn't hesitate. We got so drunk, let go of all our professionalism, and made one of those legendary nights that still lives online as grainy archival footage. I don't regret a single minute of it, because that weekend Missy became my friend for life.

When we were in Daytona, Missy mentioned that she had a record in progress that she wanted me to hop on. I was so flattered that she would want to work with me. I didn't know if she was just trying to be nice and feeding me industry lip service. But she was dead serious. A few days after we left Spring Bling, I was back on the road, and she called to formally ask me to be a feature on "One Minute Man." As soon as I heard the title, it clicked why she wanted me on it. The song is about separating the good sex from the bad, a topic that fit right into my musical catalog. I wanted to meet the Missy standard, and she was on a deadline to get the song done. She wanted me to send the verse as soon as possible, but I'd just come down with a horrible cold, complete with a stuffy nose. My voice was even more nasally than normal. The timing couldn't have been worse. I started working on the verse on the road, but I waited until I was back in Miami to record it. I still wasn't feeling any better, and my voice hadn't bounced back. But it was now or never.

The day after I sent the verse off, Missy called. She loved it. She was raving about how using my raspy, sick voice made it even better. I thought she was crazy, but who was I to argue with Missy Elliott about what sounded good? Then she told me they were shooting the video the following week, so I had to make my way to Los Angeles.

When I walked onto the set, I was immediately blown away. It was like I'd stepped into a different world. The crew had built a hotel set that could have been straight out of *Alice in Wonderland* or a sex-dungeon fantasy. All the colors were super rich, from the murals on the walls to the carpet. I shot two scenes decked out in emerald green. The first one was in the hallway as a sexy housekeeper wearing a corset and skirt. *She had access to any room in the hotel—which one would she choose?* They'd painted the dancers gold and strapped them to the walls so they'd look like statues coming to life. In the other scene, I wore a sparkling bra top and shorts set to wind my waist on a round bed that rotated around the room. In that role, I was the ultimate seductress, controlling the bedroom on my own time. That's why all the clocks were melting. Missy had such a clear vision for the shoot, giving me pointers on how to move and engage the camera, right alongside the director. I left that shoot understanding the true depth of her genius.

Missy embraced me like we were old friends from the moment we met. A light like hers can't be contained, and it's brought love and friendship into my life beyond the two of us. I met the extremely talented R & B legend Monica through Missy. Monica started working in the music industry when she was a teenager, but she stayed true to her Atlanta roots and kept it real as an around-the-way girl like me. Our mutual respect for each other made it easy for us to get along once we were connected through Missy, and the three of us have made memories that I will never forget. Like the time they pranked me for my birthday weekend.

I flew to LA with my friends Camari and Tawanna to celebrate. The plan was to meet up with Monica, Eve, and Missy to party like only we knew how. I called and texted all of them when I landed but couldn't get in touch with anybody. We checked in and got settled into my hotel suite. It had its own living room and bedroom with a luxurious bathroom and a huge tub. A balcony overlooking the city connected the rooms.

Rather than waste the day waiting around for the rest of the girls, I suggested we hit the town to get food and shop. A security detail tagged along with us to the mall, then Rodeo Drive, and finally the strip on Melrose. I was in a great mood, buying stuff for myself and my friends. I didn't know those same friends were mischievously plotting on me the entire time.

Missy finally called me back as we were arriving at the hotel. She was on her way, and she'd heard from Monica, who had to handle a few things before meeting up with us. I also got a text from Eve that she'd landed. Everything was falling into place, and I was getting excited. I looked over all the clothes I bought, trying things on I might want to wear that night and packing everything else away. I decided to take a bath, and Missy arrived while I was still in the tub, so Camari let her in and kept her company until I was done. I was back and forth between the living room and bedroom, trying to get dressed and enjoy the hotel pregame with everyone else at the same time. I was almost done and let everyone know I was ready to hit the streets. But Missy stalled. "Have you heard from Mo?" she asked. I went back into the bedroom to add finishing touches to my look and call Monica. Still no answer.

All of a sudden, I heard someone banging hard on the living room door. I decided to let someone else answer it, and then it happened again, even louder. Camari peeked his head in from the balcony door, acting concerned and asking if I could hear the pounding. "Yeah, they're knocking like the police," I told him.

We went to inspect the living room where Missy sat looking just as hesitant and confused. Tawanna was still on the balcony. Camari opened the door to two big, buff police officers and a third man who looked like the head of hotel security or some kind of private investigator. The sight of law enforcement made me stiffen up. The third guy took the lead. "We're looking for Katrina Taylor," he said.

I had no reason to lie. "I'm her. What is this regarding?"

"Were you on Melrose today?"

"Yes. What's the problem?" I motioned to some of the bags in the room and confirmed that I'd spent the day shopping. I wanted to know what the problem was, but he kept firing off questions.

"Were you with anybody else?" he asked.

I called for Tawanna, wanting to get to the bottom of whatever this was so I could continue my night. She shuffled into the room, and he turned his attention to her.

"Were you on Melrose with her today?" he asked. Tawanna told him she was. "Did you happen to steal anything when you were there?"

To my absolute shock, Tawanna mumbled, "Yeah," with the most pitiful look on her face.

What the fuck?! I scanned the room in confusion and frustration. The police were at my door to bust my friend for stealing—in front of Missy Elliott! I was so embarrassed. I tried to run some damage control and told the officer I had receipts for every purchase we made. But he wasn't hearing any of it.

"I need you both to come with me." As he said it, one of the officers stepped closer, grabbed my arm, and started to turn me around. The situation was going from bad to worse, and I burst into furious tears and let my emotions take over.

"Wait a minute—I didn't do anything!" I was still trying to talk some sense into these men. "I have all my receipts!" He ignored me, and that made me indignant. "Do you know who I am?! I'M TRINA! I got money—I don't have to steal shit!" With both hands now behind my back, I was desperate. "Camari, call my mama!" In the chaos, I hadn't noticed Missy trying to hold back fits of laughter.

At the exact moment I expected to be handcuffed, I heard a loud *boom* from a speaker I couldn't see, followed by blasting dance music. The officer let me go, and when I spun around, both he and the other buff one ripped their shirts off and started dancing. From behind them, the hotel door swung open again, and Monica walked in, cackling and grinning from ear to ear.

In the movies and TV shows, a surprise stripper prank is funny and lighthearted, but I was livid. Their script had been so realistic. They even had copies of my and Tawanna's IDs printed out to prove they knew it was us. (That was part of the ruse Camari concocted with a sales associate while I was in a fitting room.) One minute I thought I was about to be put into a squad car on my birthday weekend, and the next minute these men were picking me up and bending me over to grind all over my butt. I relaxed just enough to let the dancers do their jobs, but I kept shooting Monica and Missy horrible looks because I couldn't wait to lay into them.

Once I calmed down, the rest of the night was amazing.

Missy booked a private dinner at a restaurant and invited Janet Jackson. I grew up watching Janet on *Good Times*, dancing to "Rhythm Nation," and thinking her Velvet Rope Tour was some of the sexiest shit I'd ever seen. I was absolutely humbled to meet her. Eve joined us later, and we went to a couple of parties. Monica, Missy, and the rest of my friends made it an epic night.

The first time I was ever on MTV's *Sucker Free*, La La Vazquez was the VJ and host. *TRL* was the network's main countdown show, where crowds of teenagers from the suburbs stood outside in Times Square trying to get a glimpse of a celebrity and maybe even end up on TV. *Sucker Free* was the network's opportunity to capture the hip-hop crowd. La La was new, but she was a natural on camera, full of energy and personality. She was vibrant, funny, and not above being silly when the mood called for it. She even had me laughing and feeling good when I stepped on set. I liked this girl from the moment I met her. After the show, I invited her out to dinner with my crew.

What was supposed to be one meal turned into us hanging out together for an entire week in NYC while I was hosting events and parties to promote my second album. She hadn't been living in the city long enough to get settled in. Finding an apartment in Manhattan was stressful and expensive. When we met, she'd found one that she wanted, but she still needed another grand to get it. She wasn't asking for help, just venting. But I really believed in her and wanted her to be able to keep climbing in her career, so I gave her the money she needed. I've never regretted it.

La La is the kind of person who asks how you're doing and actually wants to know the answer. It doesn't matter how many months have gone by, with our hectic schedules, since we last spoke—she always asks for a full play-by-play of everything she's missed. She's the person you can trust to keep your secrets locked in a vault. We hang out without wigs or makeup and talk about our goals, dreams, and hardships for hours. She is usually one of the first people to reach out and check in when I'm going through something hard. She wants to know how I'm feeling, how she can support me, and she comes through every time. When she was pregnant with her son, I rearranged my schedule so that I could be in New York to take care of her and make sure she was comfortable. That was the only time I've known her to be in a bad mood. She was irritable and would cry at the drop of a dime when she was pregnant, but it was a privilege to be there for her during such a special time. I know she would have done the same thing for me.

Building my tribe of women in the industry is one of the best things I could have done for myself. Women have always been a huge part of my life. I've always looked up to them. I've always trusted and respected them. I could always count on them to pour into me. Women have stood by my side through some of the best and worst moments of my life. I don't know if I would have kept pushing in this industry if it weren't for women like Eve, Missy, La La, Monica, and some of my other girls. It's harder to build genuine relationships in a world that moves primarily online, but I know it's always worth trying.

Chapter
14

I never liked the idea of being average, so I knew I couldn't stay in that comfort zone. I had a couple of hit songs and a little bit of success, but I wanted to find my full potential as an artist. I had further to go, and I needed to do something different if I was going to get there. I had my eyes on a bigger prize. I was "going after the big man" symbolically. We followed a simple formula to make "Nann" and *Da Baddest Bitch*. We used catchy Southern beats and talked about the lifestyle of people from the streets. That kind of music will always resonate because it's raw and energetic. But there were a lot of hip-hop artists playing with different sounds and styles of music, and I wanted to expand my sound for the second album.

Missy was the first person I asked to send me a record for *Diamond Princess*. The album that "One Minute Man" was on went platinum a few months after it was released and won two Grammys for best rap solo performance and best female rap solo performance. She was already a legend, known for introducing talented new artists to the world and innovative music videos and tracks. If there was anyone who could help me take my sound to a different space, it was her.

She was working out of the Hit Factory in Miami, where music legends like Gloria Estefan, 2 Live Crew, and Aretha Franklin laid their tracks. She was already in her zone when I got there, tweaking controls and nodding along to the music playing in one of her signature track suits. I heard vocals coming from the speakers that sounded like velvet. She told me it was Tweet laying a song in another booth. Tweet's voice sounded even smoother without all the music and mixing on top of it, and I loved it. I knew I was right where I needed to be.

"What kind of song you trying to do?" Missy asked. She was a master at work, though, so she was prepared. She played four or five different beats to gauge my reaction to them. Once she had a feel for the kinds of sounds I was drawn to—futuristic, melodic—she pulled up one that she knew I would like. She didn't miss. I'm not the kind of person who can write in the studio (it's too cramped and uninspiring), so I took it with me so that I could work on it. I came back to lay the vocals and build the track. The final product ended up being "Rewind That Back."

Missy is going to be on my album, I thought to myself. *I've really made it.* I was truly honored to have a single with her. We were just about finished when she surprised me with another song she'd been working on, with Tweet singing the hook. I was grinning from ear to ear as Missy went right back into professional mode to make sure it was perfect. Two hours later, "No Panties"—a song about men not being cheap and working for the chance to be with you—was done. It was nasty, but it was bossy, and it didn't sound like the other records the guys at the label were sending.

I'd already told Slip-N-Slide straight up, "I'm not trying to make another *Baddest Bitch*." They didn't necessarily like the position I was taking, because the Trina brand they wanted had been locked in, and I was exactly where they wanted me to be. They didn't want me to switch up my style so soon. I could see the confusion and skepticism when I referenced new styles and sounds I wanted to try. Record labels are all about business and making a return on what they invest into artists. If they know one thing works, they want artists to keep producing that thing over and over again, until they find something else. It's all about a bottom line. I navigated that restriction for the first time working with Missy on *Diamond Princess*.

Trick was super vocal about me staying true to who I was. He didn't think my new music would be relatable if it lost too much of the gritty street element. My songs motivated hood chicks to get ahead in life and get everything they could from these dudes in the process. While Lil' Kim, Foxy Brown, and Eve had done this for the East Coast, I was the first solo female rapper from the South to step into the spotlight at this level.

He thought I had to stick to the same sound to send the same message, but I disagreed.

I stood firm on my position, too. Before I got in the studio with Missy, I did "Told Y'all" with Ross. But I didn't love it, because it felt too similar to stuff I'd done on the first album. Ice Cube was working on a new movie, *All About the Benjamins*, set in Miami and wanted me to send him a song for the official soundtrack to give it some hometown spice. I gave him "Told Y'all," thinking it was more fitting for a motion picture than my new album.

My label really held my hand and guided me through the process of making my first album and going on tour, but I became adamant about leading the direction of *Diamond Princess*. When I heard the "How We Do?" beat from Just Blaze, I knew that I wanted a rapper with East Coast swagger on it. Fabolous's voice has a soothing quality on any track he's on. He was popping on the charts, so my team was just as excited to get a verse from him. Ludacris returned the favor from "What's Your Fantasy?" with a feature on "B R Right." The same producer who did "B R Right" also did the beat for "Do You Want Me?" I fell in love with the heavy violins and the warped samples that combined old-school vibes with something fresh. It was that signature sound that took Kanye West from new producer on Roc-A-Fella records to megastar. It was perfect for what I was trying to do with this project.

If it had been up to me, every song on *Diamond Princess* would have been part of the new music wave I was on. But working with labels is give-and-take. This means collaborating with people in their network and using their creative ideas, even if that's not always in line with what you want to do. When I first started, I naïvely thought that artists could just choose who they wanted to make songs with, call them up on the phone, and get it done. Occasionally it really was that simple, which is how I got to work with Missy. But most of the time, you have to compromise.

In this case, that meant *Diamond Princess* would still have songs that were considered more "on brand" for me. Cool & Dre were the hottest new producers out of Miami. They'd just worked on two of Fat Joe's albums and gave my album a dynamic street edge. Signature did what he does best and added that Miami flair to "Hustling." They also put "Told Y'all" on the album and billed it as the first single, since *All About the Benjamins* was killing it at the box office and helping to push the song. *Diamond Princess* finally got the green light, and it dropped in August 2002.

With a bigger budget, I hired Misa Hylton—the stylist who was helping bridge the gap between hip-hop and fashion with artists like Lil' Kim and Mary J. Blige before I ever thought about rapping—to do creative direction and styling for the *Diamond Princess* cover. She picked this white fur bikini and accessorized it with dainty diamond jewelry. My hair was pressed and slightly windblown. Everything about that cover was soft and feminine, but still sensual. It was perfect.

The singles from *Diamond Princess* were doing well, and I

knew I had to keep that energy with the visuals and the show when I took it on the road. Because I was the only woman on my label, it was hard for the men to accept how much more it cost to execute full-glam moments. I couldn't just put on a T-shirt or jersey and a chain to sell the version of Trina that we had built up. I needed more money for hair, makeup, wardrobe, and even dancers. I was flaunting a life of luxury and expensive taste that women aspired to, so I had to look the part.

In 2002, it took a lot of work to promote an album. Radio spots, live and televised performances, talk shows, magazine interviews, and cross promotion on popular shows and box-office movies. I was doing it all. Press was always tricky because I'd done interviews before where my words were misconstrued, taken out of context, or just used incorrectly. When I was still promoting "Nann" with Trick, so many outlets wanted to play up sexual chemistry between us, which was the biggest joke since he was like a brother to me. This time around, the fixation was on my body. Photographers only wanted to dress me in skimpy outfits or bikinis—something so many female artists have to deal with—and pose me from behind.

I've always been intentional about the way I carry myself. I want to be regarded as someone deserving of respect, because I am. How I present myself is part of that. I've never been ashamed of my body or being seen as a sex symbol, but I have certain boundaries. Even when I worked at the strip club, I made it clear that I wasn't desperate and had morals. If I could evolve my sounds, I could also work to shift my narrative. I started putting my foot down on certain shoots. I would refuse to pose from the back, I declined certain wardrobe pulls, and I learned how to respond to questions that felt too sexual or irrelevant. But more than anything, I learned to take all the media hype with a grain of salt.

We ended up shooting the video for "Told Y'all" with help from the movie's production company, but Atlantic cut a check for the lead singles "No Panties" and "B R Right." I flew out to LA to film "No Panties" with Tweet. After Missy connected us, we stayed in touch and I was happy to offer advice about being a brand-new artist in the industry. When we were in the studio with Missy, it was a serious work environment. We got to let loose and be silly on the video set, which involved us dissing very sexy men in favor of diamonds and shopping. It was flashy and over the top, which I loved. Ludacris flew to Miami to shoot "B R Right" at the brand-new Diplomat Resort in Hollywood, Florida. The premise was that we took over the hotel, terrorizing the bougie guests, who looked down on us as young people with money and energy to match. My favorite scene is the one with me laid out on the penthouse terrace in a robe and head towel, getting a manicure. The video was a perfect mix of my opulent vibes and Luda's silly side, with my city as the backdrop.

.... ◆ ....

When I finished working on *Diamond Princess*, a producer approached me about starring in a movie. It was about a group of women coming together to withhold sex from their gang-banging men to stop violence in Liberty City. He thought I would be perfect for the lead role. I didn't have any acting experience and wasn't sure I had the chops for it. But playing the lead in my first-ever movie was too good of an opportunity to not at least try. When the script was sent to me, I was so overwhelmed thinking about how I would memorize all my lines that I almost quit on the spot. It felt tedious and awkward to me, but I'd already committed and couldn't back out. I kept the script with me and read through it every chance I got until it was time to film. I still didn't have my lines completely down.

A Miami Tail is a hood comedy that didn't have a big budget. I had to shoot all my scenes in a few days. I was so relieved that Sommore was my costar. She's a hilarious comedian who I'd featured on my album, and she had more acting experience than I did. She gave me a few tricks on set to teach me how to improvise when I needed to get through a scene. Some other people I knew from Miami—like my friend and fellow rapper Mr. Cheeks and silly-ass comedian Benji Brown—had also been cast in it, and they kept me laughing and in good spirits the entire time. I left the set feeling more confident about acting and wanting to be in front of the camera more.

.... ◆ ....

"That whole front row look like a gay club!" That's what Missy told me after watching one of my shows from backstage. She wasn't wrong. After *Diamond Princess* came out, the LGBTQ presence at my shows and events was noticeably bigger. They were in the crowds singing the words the hardest, wearing custom shirts with my face on it, and gassing me up to the fullest. For years I was one of the only hip-hop artists at my level happily booking performances at different Pride cele-brations, festivals, and gay clubs. I've never done one of those gigs and not had a good-ass time.

Before I ever entered the industry, some of my closest friends and family members were gay, and we always had nothing but mutual respect for each other. My uncle Perry, the one who taught me how to twirl the baton and did hair at my mom's shop, played a formative role in my life. He encour-aged all my sass and extra-ness. He wanted me to be strong and think I was the shit. I loved listening to B's stories at the nail shop. Some of the folks who work for me today are on the queer spectrum. There's a huge gay scene in Miami, where sensuality and pleasure on your own terms are nothing to be ashamed of. There are the hood gays, the Latin gays, the rich South Beach gays, and everybody in between. My exposure to and comfort with the LGBTQ community aren't things I have in common with a lot of my hip-hop peers from the South, especially men. I know firsthand that a lot of the homophobia in the industry comes from a place of ignorance. Some of the guys in my generation went from not knowing a single gay person to making their money in an industry where there are people from different backgrounds and orientations. It sucks when they can't overlook people's personal choices to really appreciate the creativity and influence of that community.

I'm always tapped into the rainbow. Not only has the queer community been a loyal fan base, but they have top-tier taste. There isn't a single great female artist that doesn't have a substantial LGBTQ audience, and there's a reason for that. My sex appeal is a selling point for men and queer women. My confident approach on how to deal with men is a selling point for women. My unapologetic attitude, especially when it comes to sex, got the attention of gay men. When I tapped into my *Diamond Princess* era, where I was serving feminine glitz and glam, they locked in. I knew I was doing what I was supposed to do when I had their support. I wanted to give them even more.

Chapter 15

Cash Money Records really did take over the '99 and the 2000. Juvenile, Mannie Fresh, Big Tymers, and Lil Wayne—their youngest artist—had the whole industry in a choke hold. You couldn't be a touring rapper in the early 2000s without running into them. They had the same pull in New Orleans that Slip-N-Slide had in Miami, so whenever I was in the Big Easy, they were the friends I would hit up. That's how I originally met Wayne.

In 2005, I heard he was in Miami before I actually heard from him. Not only was he one of the infamous Hot Boys, but he was also a solo artist growing in popularity after the release of *Tha Carter*. People spotted him around the city, and word spread that "Tha Carter" was calling Miami home. When he texted me, it was completely random.

I'm in your city, let's go out.

The message sat unanswered until a few weeks later. I was scheduled to host an event at a club called B.E.D. and knew it would be his speed. It was an upscale venue with grown and sexy vibes. The VIP sections had literal beds in them, and we would take our shoes off and pile onto the mattresses. It was a hell of a workout trying to dance on them, but it made the experience unique. I hadn't seen Wayne in a while and wanted to be as hospitable to him in my city as Cash Money was to me when I was in New Orleans. The least I could do was make sure he had a good time.

A few hours into the event, he showed up with Mack Maine and another friend. They headed straight toward my section. I watched the crowd part as security ushered them through, and when he made it to me, we hugged tightly, like the old friends we were. I had to walk around and take pictures to fulfill my obligations for the event, but I made sure we were able to catch up. He was still the chill, thoughtful guy I remembered. He wasn't forward or flirty, but at the end of the night when our crews left, he told me I could hit him up any time. There was a sincerity I hadn't noticed earlier. We went to separate vehicles, and before I could even pull off with my friends, my phone pinged with a message:

You got in the wrong car.

I craned my neck around to see if he was still in the area. He was sitting in a big-ass Rolls-Royce behind us. *I definitely got in the wrong damn car*, I thought to myself. But all I said was:

LOL

Wayne wasn't going to let me off the hook because I sent three little letters. He is supersmart, articulate, and he has a way with words that is poetic. I've recycled some of the stuff he's said to me and let my friends use it to bag guys they wanted. His game is *that* damn good.

For real, let's do something. My place, your place, Bahamas, St. Tropez...whatever you want to do.

He was flexing and dead serious. I was intrigued, but I also had my reservations. I didn't respond.

Every week or so after that I got another invitation from him to meet or go somewhere. Sometimes I was genuinely busy or out of town, but I was also unsure if I should accept. I had only ever been around Wayne in public settings, usually at a party with other people around. He was younger than me, he kept a blunt within arm's reach, and I wasn't sure how compatible we were. I had no clue what to expect from him in any kind of intimate setting. I wasn't naïve and knew how men could be. I didn't want to put myself in an uncomfortable situation, or worse—have beef with Wayne and ruin our friendship and his relationship with the city. I admired his persistence, though, and eventually it won out.

When I finally accepted his invitation to come over, I intentionally wore a casual outfit that was cute but not too sexy—just a pair of fitted jeans and a top. Assuming other people would be there, I brought one of my homegirls with me. I wanted to manage his expectations as much as I possibly could. We got closer to his door, and I didn't hear a lot of noise. When he swung it open, Wayne was standing alone in front of a beautiful plated dinner set up for two. He'd planned an intimate meal in an attempt to impress me, and it worked. I was so embarrassed that I'd brought my friend along. I wanted to toss her right off the balcony and start over. Wayne didn't trip at all. He pulled out an extra plate, and the three of us ate together.

This man was clearly serious about pursuing me, so the least I could do was give him a chance. When he hit me up again the next week, I made sure I was available. We went out to a restaurant alone and had our first official date. I paid closer attention to his mannerisms and communication style. His conversations were so refreshing because he's a true intellectual. He was not one for small talk and wasn't afraid of the heavy topics.

I was used to being wined and dined by men, but Wayne could do it on a whole new level. He wasn't trying to flex on me to make me feel like I needed him, and he wasn't trying to buy my attention. He sincerely wanted me to feel good and loved. I did. Things moved admittedly fast between us. We fell head over heels in love within a few weeks and started spending all our free time together. I had a condo in Aventura, and he had a spot in South Beach. I kept my place but was basically living with him within a month.

Wayne was affectionate and the king of grand gestures. He kept telling me he was going to get my name tattooed on himself because I meant so much to him. He couldn't wait to show me the TRINA tatted on his left ring finger. I thought it was so special and sweet. The significance of where he placed the tattoo wasn't lost on me, but I was still shocked when Wayne proposed. In true Libra fashion, he was living in the moment, but he needed it to be a huge romantic display. I had just finished a show in Houston and my crew was packing up before heading to the hotel when someone knocked on the greenroom door. I had no clue who it was, but when my friend opened it, Wayne was on one knee with a ring and some roses. I froze. Then the tears came. I was so happy that I couldn't speak—I just melted into his arms on the floor after my knees gave out. The answer was obviously yes. I loved him deeply and didn't doubt that we were going to spend the rest of our lives together.

As soon as I got back to the hotel, I went straight to Camari's room with tears still in my eyes to tell him what he'd missed. He was hanging out with a few of my dancers and they were just as happy as I was.

We had a few days off before our next show, and I was looking forward to spending them with my new fiancé, but it was hurricane season. A lot of the flights to Miami were being cancelled, so some of my team couldn't get home. But nothing was going to ruin my moment. I left them my credit card so they could extend the hotel reservation, order room service, and buy whatever else they needed while they waited out the storm. I hopped on Wayne's bus so that we could enjoy our first few days as an engaged couple. Once he proposed, I even followed through and got a tattoo of my own.

When it was time to hit the road to promote my third album, Wayne basically came with me. It was the first tour that required a rented bus to accommodate a bigger team, but Wayne owned his own tour bus and hired someone to drive it with mine. After my shows, I put my security, dancers, DJ, and the rest of the crew on my bus, and I hopped on his. He was the feature on my lead single, so performing our song together became the perfect cover to hide the fact that we were a new couple very much still in the honeymoon phase of a whirlwind romance.

Neither of us wanted our relationship to be a public spectacle in the media, so we didn't announce our engagement. But you couldn't hide anything from Wendy Williams. That fall, I was prepared when I sat down for one of her infamous interviews at 107.5. I made sure my hair, makeup, and outfit were on point because if she found anything she could use to trip me up, she would. I already knew how to answer questions that were too personal and controversial and thought I was ready for whatever she threw at me. She's good at what she does, though, and she got me to say something that confirmed Wayne and I were engaged. That one slip is how word got out we were together, and it blew up. Some people were calling us a power couple, some people were surprised that "Little" Wayne had bagged "the baddest bitch." We didn't feed into any of that because our brand personas didn't have anything to do with who we were in each other's lives. We were best friends. We were family.

When we started dating, Wayne had a six-year-old daughter, Reginae, with his ex-wife. I loved watching how hard Wayne went for his kid. He always made sure he was there for her no matter what. I adored that little girl. Whenever she was in town visiting, I tried to make sure we had everything on hand that would make her comfortable and happy, especially the fun, girly stuff her dad might have overlooked—like cute pajamas with matching slippers.

Christmastime was coming up the first time I met Reginae's mom, Toya. Trying to make a good impression, I bought Reginae so much stuff: clothes, shoes, toys—everything. She was so excited to tell her mom and show her all the gifts. Toya entertained her daughter's excitement, even though we both knew I had gone a little overboard with the shopping. "Aw, that's nice," she said to her daughter. Toya was doing her best not to make meeting her ex's new girlfriend awkward, and Reginae wasn't helping by giving an inventory of all the unnecessary gifts I had purchased. I sensed her irritation growing by the minute. Then Wayne chimed in.

"Nae needs her hair done."

That was the final straw. Toya turned the sarcasm all the way up and said, "Let the baddest bitch get it done!" Wayne didn't even bother trying to argue with her about it. I kept quiet and let them resolve the issue among themselves.

Reginae is a beautiful young woman now, and her mom

and I have laughed about that day we met. Even though Reginae isn't my child, I never took the bond we built for granted.

········ ✦ ········

Sometimes the word *genius* is thrown around just to describe somebody who is good at what they do, but Wayne is an *actual* genius. One night while I was soaking in a bath, he walked into the bathroom and sat on the edge of the tub. He started reciting some lines he'd come up with. I couldn't tell if it was a poem or a song, but it was some of the deepest shit I'd ever heard. He explained some of the meanings, and I couldn't believe that this level of creativity could just pour out of him like that. I couldn't do anything but stare at him and wonder, *Are you a real person?* Eventually, I learned that his brain was in that mode 24/7, always imagining wordplay arrangements for different situations. He could paint colors with words (which is probably why he is so damn good at talking to women), and he didn't let that talent go to waste. Wayne would go to the studio every day if he could, and sometimes he stayed there for twelve or fourteen hours. He didn't have a bunch of women or an entourage with him all the time. He was fine if it was just him, an engineer, and the music. It was like his therapy.

The only time Wayne couldn't just create lyrics was when he was having one of his migraines. One day, I found him in our closet on the floor holding his head. That's how much pain and turmoil they caused him. I begged him to go to a doctor because it scared me so bad. But what was worse than the physical pain was how frustrated he would get when he couldn't write or produce anything. It would put him in such a bad place. This was the downside to all that genius, and I was one of the few people who could talk him through it. During our first year together, he was super frustrated with what was going on with his career. He was on a mission to prove that he was one of the greatest rappers and musicians alive, but his music was being held up by industry red tape. There was another major label interested in signing him, and he was conflicted about whether to leave his label and its CEO, Baby, who was like a father to him. My position on it was always the same: "No matter who you're signed to as an artist, Baby is your dad. There is no man in this world that you have more love for." That seemed to help him for a little while, but eventually—when he wasn't going to the studio and was in a dark place—the frustration built up again. It got to the point where he started talking about quitting the music industry altogether. It was hard for me to watch because I knew how passionate he was about making music and being an artist. That was so much of what I loved about him, and I knew he wasn't himself without it.

One day, I reached a breaking point where I couldn't stand the pity party anymore. He was ready to give up, and I couldn't let that happen. If I could have physically shaken some sense into him, I would have. But I had to take another approach. I needed to remind him who the fuck he was and make him see the same man that I saw when I looked at him. He was the person who could create out-of-this-world bangers with nothing but a blunt and a microphone. He didn't even need a pen and a notebook. He was one of the best rappers alive, regardless of what label he was signed to, and I needed him to start acting like it. I needed him to find the Wayne that was a PhD-level genius and pull him out. I went into straight drill-sergeant mode. "I know you are going through a rough situation, but you have to push through it, Wayne. You are one of one, and you're fire!" I was nearly as frustrated as he was. "Y'all are literally called the fuckin' Hot Boys! You're a Hot Boy, right?!" The more I spoke, the madder I got. "Well, turn that heat up! Light the fire! Hell, be the fire . . . Turn into a god-damn fireman!" I was full-on yelling at this point, not sure if any of what I was saying was getting through to him. He went to the studio, probably to get away from my rambling. But something I said definitely clicked. The next song he recorded was "Fireman." That record sparked his career renaissance. The Wayne that the rest of the world and I knew was back.

Chapter 16

For my third album, which I was still recording when I got with Wayne, I didn't want to have to pretend for the sake of a brand. After five years of making songs and albums, touring, and getting sponsorships, I was sitting on way more money than the advance check that I had given to Nessa. I was able to save and invest, and I could still afford to cop a new bag, chain, or car whenever I wanted. I might have been the same Trina from around the way in my heart and soul, but my bank account was affluent. My real life was something other people only fantasized about. I knew that because I used to be one of those people. Now those dreams had come true. I had finally reached my Sheila E. era, and I wanted to fully embrace and celebrate that with this project. I was going to double down on the opulence and elegance. The streets be damned. If it weren't for Prince being notoriously picky with music clearances, I would have sampled "The Glamorous Life," which he wrote and co-produced, on the album. Instead, I settled on naming the whole thing *Glamorest Life*.

This album was the epitome of grown and sexy. It was smoother and more melodic than my first two. It was less about "that action" and more about enjoying a ride. Songs like "So Fresh" with Plies and even the lead single, "Don't Trip," with Wayne were laid-back and undeniably more mature. I was still adamant about collaborating with different artists, experimenting with new sounds, and introducing more themes. My ultimate mission in this game had not changed: to make music that women connect with. As a woman, I knew that there was so much more to us than what we look like, or who wants to fuck us because of what we look like. We are sensual and sexy, but we're also humans with real feelings and emotions. I was in a new relationship and very in touch with my softer side while I was working on *Glamorest Life*. I knew the girls were going to eat it up. For my other albums, I felt like I had tucked my more emotionally vulnerable songs out of the way so they didn't throw off the entire vibe. I felt comfortable putting those kinds of tracks front and center on this album. Once again, I had to push and pull with the powers that be at my label. It was one thing for me to rap about money and glamour; they just knew I would lose my fan base if I got too emotional. I was ready to go to war with the label about doing this album the way I wanted to, and it was going to start with a battle of the sexes.

While I was touring, someone sent my team a demo track with a hook written by Teedra Moses. My manager sent it to me, knowing that it was the vibe I was going for. As soon as I heard "Here we go. Here we go again," I knew I was about to make a breakup anthem. The label was trying to get Kelly Rowland to collaborate on it, and I just knew in my heart it was going to be a smash. I met Kelly and the rest of Destiny's Child years earlier when I was touring with Trick for "Nann." Since then, Destiny's Child had blown up to become one of the most successful girl groups of all time, and all the members had started to work on their solo careers. Kelly won a Grammy for collaborating with Nelly on "Dilemma" in 2003. She was a star in her own right, with a beautiful voice. She was the perfect person for the song.

I was so excited about the record that I waited until I was home in Miami before I touched it. I wanted to give it my undivided attention. I wrote the lyrics, laid the vocals down in a few hours, and sent it to the label so they could hear the same potential I did. They saw the vision and immediately green-lit a video. Kelly was in the middle of the Destiny's Child farewell tour when she flew out to Miami to shoot it with me. I had to reactivate my acting chops to play the part of a heartbroken lover looking for answers and being comforted by her friend. Kelly was the definition of gracious and poised when she introduced herself to everybody like royalty. She told me that she'd played "Here We Go" for her group mates, and both of them liked it and encouraged her to do it. Her humility and warmth stuck with me, and working with her was definitely one of the highlights of putting the album together.

It's funny that the guys were so resistant to more emotional tracks because "Here We Go" was still a story told from the perspective of the baddest bitch. The song really translates to *This man should understand I'm a woman who knows my worth and isn't afraid to add tax and send him the bill, but here he goes with the same old bullshit. Why is he playing with me?* It's a reminder that I'm that bitch, and there are consequences for not treating me how I'm supposed to be treated. The delivery was just more vulnerable. Changing the cadence and tone offered a different perspective, but the energy was still there. I was able to prove that women weren't one-dimensional and that I could talk my shit and get my point across without saying words like *pussy* or *dick* all the time. When a song that wasn't about sex at all became one of my most commercially successful, I won that battle.

My team at Slip-N-Slide and Atlantic knew that no one wanted *Glamorest Life* to do well more than I did. They had way more faith in me to define the creative direction of the album this time around. They didn't even mind that I took a more conservative aesthetic approach with the cover shoot. I know the power a fat ass can have over both men and women, from the strip club to the music industry. *Ass like Trina* was literally a catchphrase in hip-hop at the time, and all the rappers were going out of their way to find the thickest video vixens they could. But I didn't want to lead with my backside, or any other body part, for this project. I wanted to show that I was bossed up and at the top of my game. My character and my mind are just as sharp as my curves. Instead of wearing a bikini or anything too revealing, I wore black pants and a black top with a tied-up, open front. There was minimal cleavage, because that's all I had to offer, and a lot was left to the imagination. The cover exudes power and seduction instead of sex, and thankfully, everyone was on board with it.

Chapter

17

Just like my first one, this pregnancy was unexpected and inconvenient. We weren't doing much to prevent it, but Wayne and I weren't trying to make a baby, either. My body felt off, my period was late, and I decided to take a pregnancy test on a whim, just to rule it out as a possible cause. There were two lines on the test, confirming what I suspected deep down. Immediately, my mind went into overdrive trying to figure out how I was going to hide it from the label and the fans. I couldn't cancel or change any dates for the promo tour. But what if the morning sickness or fatigue affected my performance? What excuse could I use? I could hear the executives in my head: *You can't have a baby right now. We have this and that booked for you. Your music and brand don't go with a baby on your hip.*

Professionally, I was panicking, but personally, I was

happy. That was the difference between this pregnancy and my first one. I'd matured quite a bit since then, and the idea of settling down wasn't so scary anymore. Wayne and I were planning on spending our lives together, and even if we didn't, I knew he would be a good dad. When I told him the news, he was super excited. For him, it was beautiful and poetic—all the more reason to treat it delicately and keep it in our own little bubble. We only told our mothers, my sister, La La, and a few of our other closest friends. The most trusted members of my day-to-day team also knew, since I would undoubtedly have to rely on them. I kept showing up to do my job, beaming on the inside that Wayne and I were going to welcome a life together.

On my way back home from a group of back-to-back shows, I started feeling really sick. It wasn't one specific thing that I could identify, like food poisoning or the flu; I was just feeling nauseous, dehydrated, and exhausted all at once. Then I started bleeding. I'd learned that I'm anemic (I have a low red blood cell count and low iron), so I knew that I couldn't wait to go to the hospital. By the time I got there, the bleeding was worse. I blurted out to the triage nurse that I was pregnant and needed to be seen immediately. They rushed me into an exam room for an initial assessment, then brought a doctor in. I prayed for the best, but the physician didn't have good news. I was having another miscarriage.

When I called Wayne in tears to tell him that I lost that baby, I was in hysterics. He was so calm that I wasn't sure he understood what I was saying. He wasn't the kind of person to overreact, but his calmness felt inappropriate in the face of news like this. Really, he was trying to calm me down. He kept assuring me that everything was okay, but I knew it wasn't. I was hurt and confused. Everything else in my life brought me a sense of control and accomplishment. In my career, in my relationships, even in my family, I called the shots. Although hiding the pregnancy was stressful, it was still my decision. I wanted to grow, carry, and deliver this baby into the world. But now this life had been taken from me, and I just had to accept it. I felt like a failure, something I'd never thought I'd feel, and I hated it. Only someone who has physically experienced the loss of a pregnancy will understand the sense of emptiness that overcomes you. There is no amount of money, fame, or success that makes that emptiness easier to live with once it's there. It just stays with you until it's ready to be released.

As always in this industry, the show had to go on. I had to entertain. I had to promote. I had to bring good energy to photoshoots and interviews. I had to smile and make small talk. I had to look good all the time and couldn't risk being caught with puffy or tearful eyes. I had to be sexy and confident. I had to be the complete opposite of how I was actually feeling on the inside. I cried every single day after I miscarried, but I was still moving. It's wild to think about how many cities I traveled to during that time, because I was completely absent mentally and carried nothing but sadness with me. Some days were better than others, but I never knew what kind of day it was going to be until it was over.

To make matters worse, Wayne was busy, too. He couldn't

drop everything to be with me. I would go to Arizona, and when I'd get home, Wayne would be in New York. Then he would get back from New York, and I would be gone to Cali. The quality time that we built our relationship on started feeling like a jigsaw puzzle that was missing pieces. I was devastated from my miscarriage, and I felt so alone. I've never been good at asking for help or talking through my feelings. I usually try to deal with them on my own until I'm irritated or pissed off, then it's too late. But in this case, I didn't know if addressing how I felt would have helped, because I doubted Wayne could ever fully relate to what I was going through. How could he feel the loss like I did when it didn't happen to his body? It happened to mine. He didn't have to carry that emptiness with him. We were like ships in the night, and the distance between him and me just kept growing. It was easier to keep my feelings to myself.

Nothing is ever one-sided in a relationship. Wayne was feeling the strain between us. Now that we weren't spending all of our time together, our dynamic was different. I didn't have to say I was unhappy, because it was oozing out of me. I was trying to feel normal in my own damn skin again. To do that, I had to detach from everything, including him, and go inward. That emotional distance triggered a lot of insecurity in Wayne. He tried to convince me I had nothing to be depressed about when we were so blessed with success and each other. That only made me mad. This was where his Libra and my Sagittarius didn't mesh well together, and we started having serious arguments. We fussed often and tried to make up every time, but I just wasn't feeling it. Nothing seemed to matter except the loss that I had just experienced. We were reaching the end of the road, and I just didn't have it in me to fight for us anymore.

He turned to his truest love, music, and I kept going through the motions of touring. If you want a job that will let you avoid dealing with your problems, the music industry would be perfect for you. Your problems won't go away, and your feelings won't change, but you won't have to address them head-on if you don't want to. You won't have time to sit at home and grieve. You won't be alone enough to face yourself and sort through all your emotions and thoughts. You won't be able to relax long enough and let peace work its way back in. You won't have the space to figure out how to heal and move forward. You can keep working and moving and distracting yourself from the real issues. But when you do finally decide to address them, it won't always be on your terms.

During the final phase of our relationship, Wayne and I both ended up at a venue called Miami Live with our separate crews. We were officially on the outs, and I hadn't spoken to him in a couple of weeks. As soon as I heard the DJ announce he was there, I wanted to leave. But I knew everyone would be watching my reaction, and I didn't want to cause a scene. *Maybe we can just get through the night without having to interact,* I hoped to myself. But when he got onstage and started performing one of his love songs, he rapped the words directly to me. All the emotions I was trying to keep in check started stirring up inside. I missed him so much. He called me up onto the tiny stage, and when I was there, the DJ made matters worse by playing "Here We Go." He didn't know or care about what was happening between Wayne and me. He was just taking advantage of the moment to get a live performance of one of my biggest hits. I lip-synced the words, knowing my voice would crack if I tried to speak. I looked at Wayne, the person I cared for so deeply. As soon as we locked eyes, both of us broke down and let the tears fall. I didn't care about the song or the prying eyes of clubgoers anymore. We hugged, and all our complicated feelings for each other just poured out onto the stage. A lot of people thought that interaction meant we were back together, but it was the opposite. That was the catalyst for us to finally have honest, painful conversations about our relationship. We decided to call it a wrap. I just hate that the moment that brought us to that point happened in public, instead of at home where it should have been handled.

Today I can look back at our relationship and recognize that Wayne and I just grew up and grew apart, instead of having any bitterness toward him. To this day, I have nothing but the utmost respect for him. He is one of the most visionary rappers and artists to ever live, and the years that I spent witnessing his craft up close was a once-in-a-lifetime opportunity. He's a loving father who takes care of his people. He's just a dope human being. After all these years, I can stand on the fact that he was a great chapter in my life.

Chapter

18

The relationship between Slip-N-Slide and Atlantic was already rocky before *Glamorest Life*. Issues around creative control and how to manage new talent on the roster became a sore spot for both parties, and they were planning on parting ways after all the contractual obligations were fulfilled. Atlantic reached out to me with an offer to sign with them, independent from Slip-N-Slide. Ted wanted to keep me on his roster. I had to pick a side.

Atlantic's offer was tempting because being backed by a major label meant I would have continued access to their network and resources. It was expensive being Trina the rapper. The music videos, glam, features, and production were overhead expenses that required investment to reap any reward. Atlantic Records is a big company with an almost unlimited budget to pour into their artists. The upsides were obvious, but after working with them for so long, I knew that access to those resources came at a cost. They want to recoup every dollar they spend, which can put artists in debt for years. Trying to get out of the red leads to working on projects you're not as passionate about, losing creative control, or having your projects shelved at any time. Corporate machines care about dollars, not people. It's never personal, but I knew I didn't want to be one of those artists who never got to enjoy the fruits of their labor because they owed everything to a label that didn't care if they sank or swam.

I only stepped foot in the industry because I trusted Ted and his team. Slip-N-Slide wasn't perfect, but it was home. Ted, Trick, Ross, and the rest of the guys there were my family. They protected me from a lot of oversight I would have had to navigate alone if my deal was directly through Atlantic. The reason I was able to go into some of those meetings and fight for the songs and sounds I wanted on my album was because of the relationship I had with Slip-N-Slide. If I stayed with them after they went independent, I would have way more creative control, even if the budget was significantly smaller. If my goal was to win awards, be on the radio, and play the industry game, staying on Atlantic would have been a no-brainer, but it wasn't. Being able to move how and when I wanted, with people I loved and trusted, was way more important. I knew where my loyalties lay. I declined Atlantic's offer and stayed at home where I belonged.

Always the businessman and hustler, Ted already had a plan B in the works to get me some of the backing I needed.

Slip-N-Slide signed a new distribution deal with EMI, which was one of the biggest record labels in the world before they sold to Universal. It had been two years since *Glamorest Life* dropped, and it was time for me to get back in the studio. Coming off the breakup with Wayne, I was open to doing something upbeat and light to celebrate getting back to myself as a woman. C.O. and Ted really wanted my first project with the new distributor to get back to the foundation of who I was as an artist. I was secure in my brand and knew I had fans who would tap in regardless, and I really wanted to feed them what I knew they liked.

This project wasn't about being super vulgar or being too deep in my feelings. It was more important that I captured the swag, the confidence, the grown-woman sensuality, the vulnerability, and the good energy that you have when you've seen it all, done it all, and *know* you're the baddest bitch. The guys kept calling the project *Da Baddest Bitch 2* when we were in the studio. We had crazy, intense debates about the title because I was still sensitive about regressing. I didn't want people to think I was living in the past. Everybody was aligned on the songs that were stacking up for it, and we compromised on *Still da Baddest* as the official name of the album.

Missy came through with a damn-near-perfect club anthem on "I Got a Bottle." We wrote it based on our real experiences of clubbing, getting drunk, and turning up together.

So full, so far gone
Forgot where I parked and lost my iPhone

We cried laughin' in the studio remembering some of the details that didn't make it onto the track. I don't care that it's a silly party song—"I Got a Bottle" will always be dear to my heart. Ross and I got back to that signature Miami sound—full of different percussions and horns—on "Hot Commodity." Some critics thought I was just trying to copy the vibes of "Here We Go," but I actually had my eye on a new boo when I was working on "I Got a Thang for You." Keyshia Cole was one of the hottest R & B singers out at the time, so of course I wanted her to come and kill the hook. *Still da Baddest* is one of my strongest projects because it's so versatile. There's literally something on that album for everybody. Unfortunately, not everyone was happy for me.

.... ◆ ....

Wayne was having problems with some of his former label-mates. They were taking shots at each other on diss records, and I was getting caught in the cross fire because without us confirming or denying our breakup, many people still assumed I was Wayne's woman. Grown-ass men were speaking on my body and relationships in an attempt to insult my ex. They didn't care if they offended me in the process. I was just collateral damage. That didn't make it any less disrespectful. It was becoming harder to stay silent while people shitted on my name, then I got a call from C.O. that was the straw that broke the camel's back.

"We're going to the studio right now!" He was aggravated and on a hundred. He told me about a magazine interview another female artist did, and in it she was talking mad shit about me. I vaguely knew who the woman was. She was a female rapper who collaborated with Trick on a couple of songs in the past. She had a popular single that dropped the same year as *Diamond Princess*. I really liked the song she did with Trick, but I'd heard through the grapevine that she had a problem with me. Rumors come with fame, so I always took a cautious approach and never fed into them unless I was mentioned by name. When I got to the studio and read the interview C.O. was talking about for myself, I was shocked. The interviewer asked her about my music, and she answered by attacking my character and morals, just like the guys Wayne was into it with. I had never met this woman, but whatever problem she had with me was clearly personal.

After eight years in the game and three albums under my belt, it was like I was being reduced to a ho with a microphone. I was pissed, and I understood why C.O. wanted me to take it to the booth. The idea of industry or internet beefs has always felt like a waste of time because where I'm from, people settle their issues on sight, in person, with hands. But I have never been afraid to speak my mind or defend myself if the situation calls for it, and I firmly believe that there is only so much disrespect you can tolerate. I'm not a battle rapper, and I never wanted to build my career on drama, negativity, or animosity with anyone else, but enough was enough. If they could talk shit, so could I.

When I sat down to write the song, I was intentional. Everyone and every situation was addressed by name so there wouldn't be any confusion. I recorded "What's Beef" and released it feeling like, *I said what I said, I meant what I said, and now I'm done with it.* Any further back-and-forth with me would need to be face-to-face. We dropped the song online, and it started getting picked up by hip-hop and gossip blogs right away. It wasn't like me to make a record like this, and everyone noticed. This was one song that wasn't about the fans, though. This was my way of addressing people who thought I would lie down and take disrespect.

The tension naturally dissolved with the guys I mentioned because most of their energy was still directed at Wayne anyway. But the lady who talked shit about me in that magazine couldn't let it go. It's been eighteen years since I dropped "What's Beef," and she still hasn't stopped. At first, I assumed she was jealous of my success or chasing clout. Unfortunately, people in my industry have been known to stir up mess with more successful artists just to benefit from the extra attention it brings. I mostly ignored her and stuck to my guns about never addressing her by name again, because I didn't want to give her a bigger platform. It's been relatively easy to do because we don't have any mutual friends, we've never run in the same circles, and we've never been in the same room. I moved on and assumed she would eventually do likewise, but she never did.

I have been a public target of her anger for nearly two decades. That's deeper than regular grudges or jealousy when we've never worked together, gone to school together, hung out, owed each other any money, or done anything to harm one another. Fans and critics have called it a rivalry, but how can it be when only one person participating knows why it exists? I've built a body of work and a legacy. She's become known for her big single and hating me. All I can do at this point is pray for her peace. I can't imagine how much of her energy has been used to keep that kind of animosity going for so long.

.... ◆ ....

There were only two songs on *Still da Baddest* that the label and I weren't on the same page about. The first one was "Look Back at Me." The guys loved that it was combative and in-your-face. This was what they had in mind when they wanted me to tap back into my foundations. It was just like "Nann," which was exactly why I didn't want to do it. I put in so much work to be able to express myself in different ways, and this song felt like taking steps backward. I didn't want to make a song just for the shock factor. But they were adamant about it, so I had to compromise. "Look Back at Me" is raunchy and over-the-top, but the fans eat it up every time I perform it.

Still da Baddest was done and turned in to the label when I got the idea for "Single Again." I was finally starting to come out of that dark place I was in after Wayne and I broke up. There wasn't any real drama between us, but the gossip blogs were making it hard for him to stay out of sight and out of mind. Every time he was seen in public with someone, the pictures would hit the internet, and they always came with different stories and narratives from people who were trying to connect the dots and decipher what happened between us. Hell, *we* were still trying to figure out what was happening with us now that we weren't a couple. That onstage debacle between us at the club was a perfect example of that. A lot of what I heard or saw online was bullshit that I could see right through. But every once in a while, something would get under my skin, and that's what happened when I decided to make "Single Again." I remember thinking, *So this is how it is? This is how niggas wanna act? Bet.* I needed to talk my shit and remind everyone I was still that bitch. I started jotting down my ideas and set up a session to record it.

The guys thought adding "Single Again" to the album was doing too much. I already had one breakup song—"Wish I Never Met You"—on the track list, and they thought a second one would change the whole vibe of the album. I kept trying to explain that "Single Again" is not a sad song, but once again, their male perspective was clouding their judgment. They couldn't imagine a woman ever feeling good enough to celebrate a breakup. I knew firsthand how liberating it can be to get back to yourself after being wrapped up in another person and it not working out. I already pictured those women: celebrating for the first time with their friends after a breakup, singing this record at the top of their lungs. Just like the last battle over "Here We Go," I could show my team of dudes better than I could tell them.

I laid down vocals for the song and hummed over the hook, thinking we would get a featured artist to execute it for the final version. The more I played with the record, the more I started singing the full words as a placeholder. Every time I was in the booth to add more layers or ad-libs, I freely belted out the words. I love melodies and R & B, but I am not a singer by any stretch of the imagination. I didn't hate hearing myself on "Single Again," though. Something about it was working. We were able to mix and engineer it to give it a little bit of an edgy pop flair. It didn't sound like anything else I had ever done, and now I was one hundred percent sure I didn't want anyone else to sing it. "Single Again" was meant to be a solo record.

Chapter
19

Funnily enough, I was actually with Wayne the first time I ever laid eyes on Kenyon Martin in person in July 2007. Wayne and I were in that weird transition phase, no longer committed but not ready to give each other the space we needed to really move on. In our defense, it was hard to make a clean break when our worlds were so intertwined. Neither of us had it in our hearts to hate each other, and sometimes it was easier to just carry on with business as usual. On this particular day, I went out with some of my friends, and Wayne came with us. I noticed Kenyon in the club because it's hard to miss anybody that damn tall. I assumed he was an athlete but had no clue who he was, so I kept it moving and had a good time with the people I came with.

A few days later, I attended a celebrity basketball game hosted by Alonzo Mourning. He was a center for the Miami

Heat, and there were many athletes or entertainers in my city I didn't know. The game was part of Zo's Summer Groove, a charity event he hosted every year to raise money for kids and families. He organized golf tournaments, concerts, and of course, all-star basketball games that his colleagues in the league gladly signed up for. It was a magical night from the very beginning.

I pulled up to the back entrance of the venue with my crew, where all the VIPs—celebrities and hoopers—were coming in. We got there at the exact same time as Dennis Rodman, and I was surprisingly starstruck. After almost ten years in the industry, meeting all kind of famous people, I rarely fangirled. But Dennis Rodman was more than a basketball player; he was a pop-culture icon. I was actually nervous and grinning like a madwoman when I spoke to him. He was so sweet and silly. He said, "Oh my God—I love you!" with a fake high-pitched voice, imitating a fan. Then he gave me the biggest hug. It was only awkward because I'm so short, and comparatively, he's a giant. I just kept smiling and craning my neck trying to look up at him. He kept his arm around me, said, "Let's go!" and we walked into the tournament together. I sat watching the game composed, but my mind was doing gymnastics trying to process the fact that I was sitting courtside next to Dennis fucking Rodman. Everybody wanted a chance to shake his hand, take a picture, or talk to him, and I didn't blame them. I probably would have sat there staring at him the whole night if it weren't for all the cameras. To not make a fool out of myself, I made sure to socialize with my friends so I didn't invade his space. We had a blast.

On the way back to my seat from the bathroom, another giant approached me. This one was younger and *very* handsome. He reached for my hand. "Hi, I'm Kenyon."

I gave it to him. "Hi, I'm Trina."

Smiling, he said, "I know who you are." Kenyon was smooth, and I liked that.

We discussed our plans for after the game, and he suggested my friends and I roll through an event he had to attend. That's what we did after the game ended and I hugged Dennis Rodman one more time. Kenyon found his way over to our section, and I finally got to learn a little more about this mystery man. He was from Dallas and played for the Denver Nuggets, but he loved to do weekends in Miami during the offseason. He was cool and easy to talk to, but we could only talk so much. Neither of us wanted to give the blogs anything to start speculating about, so we kept it brief at the function. We discreetly exchanged numbers and agreed to continue our conversation privately. It wasn't until we were leaving that one of my friends reminded me: "Isn't that the same guy from the club the other night?"

Kenyon left Miami within a few days to enjoy the rest of his time off. I was still trying to get emotionally untangled from my ex. I wasn't looking for a relationship, but I knew I'd hear from him again. I called my homegirl La La. She was living with her then fiancé, Carmelo Anthony, who was Kenyon's teammate on the Nuggets. She'd given birth to the baby boy that made her so emotional during pregnancy, and they were all settled in Denver. If there was anything important about Kenyon that I needed to know, she would be the one to tell me. She had no red flags to point out, so when he finally called a few weeks later, I answered. For months, Kenyon and I connected exclusively through phone calls and text messages, which gave me time to wrap up my album and my feelings for Wayne. On his end, the preseason began, so neither of us felt pressure to hurry things along. Not having physical access to each other was a great way to really get to know one another and build a foundation.

I didn't see Kenyon in person again until the wintertime. He invited me to Denver for one of his home games and to celebrate my birthday with me. I couldn't wait to see him again, and I was even happier that I could spend time with La and her baby while I was there. I headed straight to the game as soon as I hopped off the plane, and I sat courtside with my girl. We barely watched the game because we were caught up talking, eating, cracking jokes, and dying laughing. Afterward, Kenyon and I went to dinner for our first official date. The few months we spent talking left no question that we had deep feelings for each other. That first date was the beginning of our relationship.

To understand how much I loved Kenyon, you have to understand how much I hate the cold. Nothing about my Caribbean blood or my Miami roots is set up for temperatures under forty degrees, and I still regularly traveled to Denver to be with him during the winter and spring. It was easier for me to visit him than it was for him to come to Miami. The lifestyle of athletes is completely different from that of rappers. This was my first time ever seriously dating a professional athlete, and the rules he had to abide by in his industry were way stricter than mine. Athletes have to be so regimented with everything. Their success relies on what they eat, how much sleep they get, how hard they go in the gym, and how long they spend practicing. Basketball players are part of a huge corporate organization—the NBA—that always keeps them on a tight schedule of games, press conferences, and events. Not to mention commitments from endorsements and brand deals. It's very buttoned-up, by the book, and strict. Music artists, even those signed to major labels, don't have to work under the rank of coaches, team owners, and league guidelines that keep track of everything we do. When I was with Wayne, we felt free to do whatever we wanted. Someone was always a phone call away to make last-minute changes to our schedules. We could party all night and sleep in until the afternoon, show up late to photoshoots, leave events early, hop on a flight to a different city one night and fly back the next morning. I wasn't used to having a partner who had to be so focused in work mode, but I understood Kenyon's limitations. So I braved the cold to make sure we got quality time with each other.

As we grew closer, Kenyon hated when it was time for me to leave. I was part of his escape from the stress and pressure of his job, so I tried to be with him as often as I could. Eventually, he thought it made more sense for me to just move in, and I was not into the idea at all. Not only is Denver cold as hell, but it's also a totally different world with a pace of living I wasn't used to. In some ways, it's the complete opposite of Miami, New York, or LA, where there is always something happening. Denver was very much turned down. Even if there was more to do, it was usually too cold for me to even think about leaving the house. But the time zone difference and our hectic schedules made it hard for Kenyon and me to stay connected. We were in love and missing each other more than either of us wanted to, so I agreed to move. For the first and only time in my life, I didn't live in Miami.

The transition wasn't so bad at first. Promo for *Still da Baddest* was in full swing, and coming home to Denver meant I got to see my man and actually decompress. When I came home to Miami, I was surrounded by my friends and family and everybody else who wanted to hang out. Even though we never needed one, there was always a reason to party. And we did. Being home in Miami wasn't necessarily restful, because I had to maintain certain boundaries.

After my second album came out and I started making real money, it was nothing for me to hit South Beach and let my friends buy whatever they wanted from any store. I gave my family members money whenever they asked. All the clubbing and party-hopping my friends and I did was usually on my tab. This was years before promoters comped bottles for celebrities in exchange for exposure. I got a call from my accountant one day. He was going over my monthly transactions and couldn't identify a merchant I had multiple charges from, for thousands of dollars each. The merchant name on my bank statement didn't ring a bell, so I was just as stumped as he was. *Maybe I was a victim of identity fraud*, I wondered. He listed off the transaction dates, and I couldn't do anything but laugh when the realization hit me. They were my charges from Privé, a club on South Beach. That was my go-to spot because the music was always good, and it was a more private atmosphere. I could turn up there and stumble out tipsy without worrying about a bunch of fans or paparazzi. Every time I stepped foot inside, I got a section and a few bottles. Hearing that I'd run up nearly $70,000 in a month knocked the smile right off my face. I had spent enough money for a down payment on a decent house. It was an egregious amount of money for something so frivolous, but it was easy to do when I swiped my card for several thousand dollars at a time. Nessa was still involved in my finances, and when she found out about the Privé spending, she was more pissed than I was.

I had to ask myself how much of that had been for *my* benefit. I certainly didn't drink $70,000 worth of alcohol by myself. I thought back on some of those nights and remembered only having a drink or two but still swiping my card for thousands of dollars. I was just throwing money away for people who couldn't even reciprocate if they wanted to. I made a decision right then and there to be more intentional about my spending, especially when it came to my social and family circles.

Too many people were starting to expect that kind of treatment and spending from me. Even outside of partying, some of my family members would let their lights get cut off or fall behind on their rent because they just assumed that I would swoop in and save them. I couldn't respect or enable that kind of mess. I was not going to be giving handouts to just anybody who asked. I needed to change those expectations. You can come out with me, but you can pay for your own drinks. If you're not working, in school, or starting some kind of business venture, don't expect for me to bail you out of any financial predicaments. To this day, I have a rule about not loaning out money because I've learned the hard way that those dynamics can ruin relationships. If they don't pay me back, if I think I'm being taken advantage of, or if they feel a certain way because they think I'm clocking their money, what started as an agreement over a few dollars can turn into something so much deeper.

When I changed the way I moved with my wallet, I noticed some people switch up and keep their distance. But I was fine with that. I didn't win a billion dollars in the lottery. I had to work hard as hell for my money. If I suddenly lost it all, no one would be able to earn it back except me. I couldn't be an ATM machine for anyone except me, because I was learning I had to put a lot of my money back into my career.

Needless to say, I appreciated the seclusion Denver offered. It's a very subdued and laid-back city. People there don't seem to care about anything except weed, the outdoors, and sports. I never had to worry about paparazzi hounding me for pictures or random people pulling their phones out to record me, unless I was with Kenyon. I could walk around natural, with no makeup, by myself, and just be normal. Denver gave me the peace and quiet I needed but couldn't get in the 305. It also had a positive impact on my relationship. With Kenyon, I felt the most settled down and domesticated I ever had. That was the closest I ever got to being a housewife because . . . hell, I was always in the house.

I never got used to the weather in the winter months, and his promise of mink coats did nothing to change that. On any given evening, you could find me in the bed, under the electric blanket, with the fireplace on and the heat set to damn near ninety degrees. Or I took my time cooking elaborate meals just to enjoy the warmth of the oven and stove. With the exception of Kenyon's basketball games, I didn't dare to venture out anywhere unless it was to spend time with La. If it weren't for her, I would have been completely isolated in Denver. I am not the kind of person who can deal with sitting still and feeling confined for long periods of time. It makes me anxious. When too much snow fell and I knew the airports would cancel flights, I felt trapped, even if I didn't have any travel plans. I really struggled in the two years I lived there, but it was worth it for my person.

When Kenyon got a bright-red tattoo of my lips on his neck, I thought it was so sexy and romantic. It wasn't obvious to the rest of the world what the tattoo meant or why he'd gotten it at first. I liked having an inside thing between us. I was surprised when he disclosed to a reporter that the lips were mine, but it wasn't a secret, so I didn't mind. Both of us felt like we were in the relationship for the long haul, and we let ourselves enjoy it. I eventually got into the groove of us living together. We spent his breaks together, in his hometown of Dallas, which I loved for the climate change alone. All his family, homeboys, and friends still lived there. He was the hometown hero, and they always rolled out the red carpet for him. We had a lot of fun there. It wasn't Miami, but it was warmer and more lit than Denver.

Even though our professional lives were set up differently, the cultures still overlapped. Kenyon loves music, especially hip-hop, and would play it from the moment he woke up. Even in the shower, he had to have some music to vibe to. Rappers and athletes have a mutual respect for each other because they share similar levels of success and influence. Both industries show what's possible for young Black men with money. This is why so many athletes do cameos in music videos and why so many rappers love to be seen canoodling at the Super Bowl or sitting courtside during the NBA playoffs. I felt like Kenyon appreciated the access to the entertainment industry that came from being with me. He was excited to walk carpets, attend award shows, and meet different artists. It wasn't from an unhealthy place; it was just a refreshing break from the repetitiveness of the NBA. At these events, we weren't low-key like we were in Denver; we were a "celebrity couple."

I noticed that in interviews, people wanted to talk about my relationship, even if I was by myself. When we stepped out together, the pictures always ended up on the blogs with commenters picking apart our outfits and body language to draw conclusions about the state of our relationship. If we went out by ourselves, people speculated that we had broken up. If we went out with other people, they wondered who was cheating. Some people loved us together, and some people, especially some NBA fans after he got that tattoo, hated it. We were being compared to other couples like La La and Melo. It was like the relationship itself became its own celebrity, which was weird to me. It was wild to see a part of my life that was so personal become a topic of public conversations. I knew to keep all the hype at arm's length. It's hard enough to be in a relationship with somebody when you're both busy and working on different schedules in different places. If you let the opinions of other people into the dynamic, it'll never work. Kenyon and I had enough issues to worry about on our own without commenters being involved.

Kenyon isn't a bad person by any means. I wouldn't have been with him in the first place if I thought he was. When I was with him I felt certain he was going to be my husband one day. He was the first person I really saw myself having a traditional settled-down family life with. I love Wayne to death, but that relationship was partially fueled by the excitement of our rock star lifestyles. I wasn't living fast with Kenyon. Usually, it was my work that required us to be in front of cameras and in clubs. Watching how he and some of his colleagues moved, I understood that being an entertainer and having a lot of money didn't mean I had to be on the scene all the time. I could have a home life that was calm and normal if I wanted that. I reached another level of maturity in that relationship, and I appreciate Kenyon for giving me that different perspective.

However, he is still a man. At the time, he was a man *and* a professional athlete on one of the best teams in the NBA, traveling all around the country to crowds in the tens of thousands. I've spent my whole life around men with money and power. I know what comes with it. The temptation is real, the access that they have to women is real, and their desires are real. I've never been naïve about sex being part of the lifestyle for men in Kenyon's position. I was never the kind of girlfriend who could sit at home trying to enforce a curfew or follow his team around like a groupie just to make sure I was the only woman he was dealing with. He and I had a bond that was special, and that was the source of my trust and sense of security. However, disrespect is disrespect, and I was not the kind of girlfriend who could ever stand or tolerate that. Kenyon was unfaithful, and our entire relationship crumbled as a result.

I try not to judge women who stay with their partners through infidelity, because I know firsthand what it's like to really love someone and want the relationship to work despite their mistakes. But I know myself. Staying with someone who cheated would always have me lying in bed wondering if he really changed, if I made the right decision, or if the relationship was worth the heartache. What if he cheated again and I'd have to live with knowing he only had an opportunity to play in my face more than once because I had given it to him?

Absolutely not. I made so many sacrifices to be in that relationship and support him as his woman. This wasn't something I could just get over and move past.

When I'm in a relationship, I'm good to people, I'm accommodating, and I'm really trying to make the person happy. But don't let that soft energy fool you. When I feel disrespected or taken for granted, I am always going to remind you that I'm not the one to play with and I will leave you where you had me fucked up. It's not always easy or simple, but it's necessary. The relationship between Kenyon and me became strained, and in the end, we argued way more than I wanted to. So I left before shit went from bad to worse. After two years, I packed my belongings, left Denver for good, moved back to Miami, and never looked back.

Chapter
20

By the 2010s, the strong presence women had in hip-hop was fading. It had only been a couple of years since *Still da Baddest* hit no. 1 on the Billboard Hot Rap Songs and Hot R&B/Hip-Hop Songs charts, but it felt like female MCs had been put on a shelf. Occasionally, we'd come out on a big feature, body it, and then a bunch of dudes would take over again. After Missy dropped her album *The Cookbook* in 2005, she turned her focus on more producing and song-writing behind the scenes, occasionally hopping on a feature to support one of those records. Lil' Kim went to prison the same year. When she got out, she left her label, so she didn't have any major releases, either. My girl Eve was exploring more acting gigs. Remy Ma got her skills doing battle rap out of the Bronx and came up with Fat Joe's Terror Squad. She was killing it when she first dropped. Joe's wife, Lorena, is another one of my closest friends, and Remy and I had the same hairdresser, so we ran into each other all the time. I was on set when she shot the "Where da Cash At" video with Wayne. All of Remy's hard work was paying off for her until she caught a case and had to put her career on hold. I started working on my next album in a hip-hop landscape where songs by female rappers weren't getting the club or radio play they used to. *Amazin'* was my fifth album, a milestone only a couple of other female rappers had hit in 2010.

I started working on the project when I was still in a happy relationship, living in Denver. By the time it was done, I'd switched time zones, zip codes, relationship status, and mind-sets. I felt like the last woman standing in an action movie. I was victorious, despite everything I'd been through, and it gave me a lot of clarity. I could put an album together in my sleep by that point. I had a backlog of songs for the album that I had already laid demos for. All I had to do was start choosing which ones made the most sense and piece everything together. I only wanted songs that felt elevated, mature, and different from what people expected. If something felt fresh or innovative, I was down to try it. That's why *Amazin'* has such a wide range of features, from Lady Saw to Lyfe Jennings and Monica. Lady Gaga cowrote "Let Dem Hoes Fight" with the intention of being on the song but couldn't clear the label red tape, so we had Kalenna sing the hook. I met Nicki Minaj after Wayne signed her to his label, Young Money. I instantly understood what Wayne saw in her as an artist. She was super creative and ready to go to the top from day one. She was the complete opposite of me when I came into the industry, just going with the flow and figuring it out as I went. Nicki was still in her mixtape era when we met, but she had the streets going crazy. Her flow was nasty, and she used it to rap circles around so many of her male peers. She gave women, especially younger female fans, something to look forward to in hip-hop, and they latched right onto her. We were both featured on a Yo Gotti remix called "5 Star" with Gucci Mane in 2009 and shot the video with them in LA to create some more buzz for it. She was extremely humble when we met and told me how much respect she had for me as a woman in the game. From that moment on, I was rooting for her.

Gotti premiered the "5 Star" video on BET's *106 & Park*, and it went no. 1. That song has become another one of my hood classics. Play it today and it still goes hard. Real fans of mine, Nicki's, Gucci's, or Gotti's are always going to mention that record when they talk about our iconic verses. Just like "Nann," "5 Star" was a moment for the streets, but I don't think it would have that same magic if there were only dudes on it. I knew I wanted to work with Nicki again, so I made sure she was on the list of features for *Amazin'*.

"Million Dollar Girl" was the only Slip-N-Slide video that cost more than "Da Baddest Bitch." The song featured Keri Hilson and Diddy, so Ted knew we had to open our wallets and go all out for the visuals. We rented a plane hangar at Miami-Opa Locka Executive Airport, where private jets land and take off.

We used one area as a huge green-screen stage to film scenes of me as a super glam casino hostess, and Keri and me as club performers. We used the other area of the hangar to shoot scenes with all three of us in and around a private jet. We went all out with the wardrobe, jewelry, hair, makeup, and production changes. Slip-N-Slide spent nearly double what they did on my first video, betting on this being a watershed moment for the label. But there wasn't much promotion for the single beyond that. We didn't book any big performances or TV spots. It seemed to me that Ted thought the expensive video and the strength of Diddy's and Keri's features were enough to take "Million Dollar Girl" where it needed to go. I knew it needed more of a push.

My favorite song on *Amazin'* when it came out was "That's My Attitude" because it really captured the mode I was in. The beat was hard enough for the streets but high-energy enough for the club. It needed a video, but the label's budget was maxed after "Million Dollar Girl." I couldn't accept that. I believed in "That's My Attitude" and refused to sit on my hands about it, so I did the whole video myself. I hired R. Malcolm Jones, a director in the city I'd been wanting to work with, to shoot it. I hired the dancers, the models, the stylists, and the glam teams. I even called my friend Bryant McKinnie—who played in the NFL—and convinced him to let me borrow his Maybach for the shoot. The video was sleek and bossy, just like I envisioned. The label was surprised at how well it turned out, and they had a newfound faith in "That's My Attitude." Most of the promotion for the song was paid for with

Trina at her birthday party with her sister, Laura, and mom.

Trina, fifth grade, at Liberty City Elementary School.

Hosting the Source Awards.

Hosting the Source Awards, Miami, Florida.

Trina with her mom doing hair at home.

Trina with niece Suga.

RIGHT: On the set of the
"Here We Go" video shoot, 2012.

BELOW: At the Source Awards,
2004, Miami, Florida.

ABOVE: "Here We Go" video shoot,
2012.

RIGHT: First performance, 1999,
at The Moon, Tallahassee, Florida.

Trina, age five, with cousin Stella, age four, at their grandma's house, Liberty City, Florida.

Trina with cousin Stella, Easter Sunday photo.

Eighth-grade prom.

On the set of Webbie's "Bad Bitch" video as a featured artist, Miami Beach, Florida.

Trina, age four, in Ballerina Dolls, Miami, Florida.

"Da Baddest Bitch" photo shoot, Miami, Florida.

Trina with her new husband, Ben.

RIGHT: Club Story, Miami Beach, Florida.

BELOW: Trina, third grade, at Liberty City Elementary School.

Trina with her sister, Laura, at their mom's shop, Liberty City, Florida.

Trina, eighth-grade prom, the night her grandmother passed away.

At sister Laura's graduation: *(left to right)* friend Pinkey, cousin Stella, Laura, Trina, and cousin Joy.

On the set of Silkk the Shocker's "That's Cool" video as a featured artist.

On the set of Webbie's "Bad Bitch" video as a featured artist, Miami Beach, Florida.

With brother Snoop at Trick Daddy's video shoot for "Boy."

Hosting the Source Awards.

Trina, age sixteen, fun photo.

Trina, age four, with cousin Stella.

Trina, age eighteen, and friends: *(left to right)* Pinkey, Trina, the cameraman, godsister Angie, and cousin Stella.

With niece Suga.

Trina, second-grade photo.

Trina, age six, at her mom's
store with cousin Stella.

At sister Laura's graduation: *(left to right)* friend Pinkey, cousin Stella, Trina, cousin Joy, and Laura.

Trina, age sixteen, fun photo at the flea market, Miami, Florida.

With brother Goonkie for his high school graduation.

With brother Goonkie.

With brother Goonkie after
his football game.

Trina at a roller-skating rink for
her birthday party with her sist
Laura, and mom.

On the set of a video shoot.

Going out with childhood
friend Pinkey.

Trina, tenth grade,
Miami Northwestern Senior
High School majorette photo.

On the set for the "Da Baddest Bitch" video shoot.

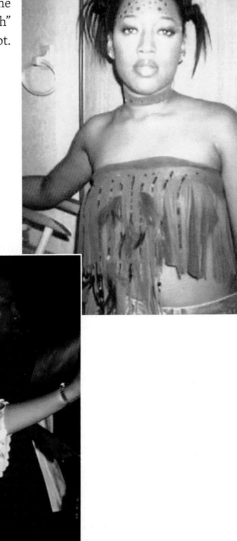

Live performance, pictured with C.O. (formerly of Tre+6).

With niece Suga at the
movie theater.

On the set of Trick Daddy's
"Nann" video shoot.

Glamorest Life photo shoot.

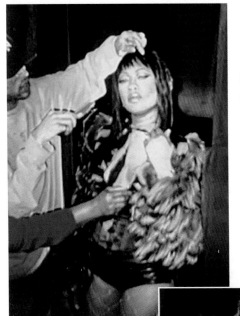

On the set of the "Told Y'all" video shoot, 2002.

Hosting the Source Awards, 2004, in Miami, Florida.

my own money, but it was okay if it meant I could execute all of it exactly how I wanted. For the *Amazin'* cover, I took the same ownership. I wanted to give Hollywood, lavish, show-girl, glamour. I handpicked the photographers, stylists, and makeup artists. I gave input and feedback on the concepts. I approved the final looks and shots. It came together perfectly, and I was proud of myself.

That's why *Amazin'* will always have a special place in my heart. It was the project that showed me what I could really do when I was determined and focused. I didn't have to rely on anybody else, because nobody had my back like I did, no-body understood me like I did, and nobody could handle all of me like I could. Investing in myself and seeing the fruits of that labor unlocked something for me. I felt more confident and independent than I ever had in my career. *Amazin'* was a symbolic moment, reflecting how far I'd come as a business-woman. I'd achieved so much success over the years, and it was glorious—it really *was* amazing. But I did it in an industry that didn't always appreciate or pour into women the way it should. Doing things on my own was a huge source of pride, but in the back of my mind, I was wondering, *If I'm doing all of this because my label isn't, why am I on this label?*

Chapter 21

As the only woman on Slip-N-Slide, I'm not sure if my label ever really understood how important branding is for female artists. Male rappers don't have to look a certain way to be accepted. They don't have to carefully fine-tune their persona to tap into different fan bases. I didn't feel like Slip-N-Slide's approach to marketing my albums ever evolved with the music. I was five albums and twelve years in, and the only budget I knew I was guaranteed to get was the cost of wardrobe, styling, and production for the cover shoot. They still seemed to think that big, splashy covers made an album sell. Other artists who have been doing this for as long as I have can document their legendary careers with a visual body of work. Iconic performances, music videos, and fashion moments tell the story of their artistry just as much as their music catalog does. There are so many songs in my career I wish I could go back and execute videos for, like "Off Glass," "Hustling," and "I Got a Bottle." There are so many performances and promotional concepts I would have loved to have executed during my album rollouts but didn't have the chance to.

None of this is a knock on Ted. He was, and still is, a great businessman. He works in facts and figures. Ted was very good at keeping checks and balances to make sure Slip-N-Slide stayed within a budget and was in position to see returns on their investments. But the music industry thrives on innovation. To be successful, you have to leave room for forward thinking and taking risks, and I felt like Slip-N-Slide wasn't keeping up. Hip-hop was changing in the 2010s. Trap was the new sound for real hood music, but it was still mostly underground, being pushed via new artists, mixtapes, and DVDs. Rap wasn't seeing the same sales that it had five to ten years before. The hip-hop tracks that were getting a lot of play on the radio and receiving award nominations were hybrid blends with pop or R & B. Artists like Kid Cudi and even Flo Rida blew up because people were hungry for different sounds. It was the perfect time to try new shit and see what could stick.

For the label, change can mean risk. From Slip-N-Slide's perspective, it was probably hard to justify making huge investments when the possibility of profit seemed so uncertain. I'd heard that Slip-N-Slide was already in a tight financial spot because of other legal issues and signing new talent. I empathized with the position Ted was in, but I felt extremely boxed in. I was the biggest artist on their roster, and after taking the lead on pretty much everything for *Amazin'*, I didn't believe they had the resources to sustain my growth moving forward. I didn't feel like I had strong creative leadership, and I was overseeing the label when it came to my drops. Everything we were doing felt a little stale and basic. Slip-N-Slide had helped me come a long way, but I didn't feel like they could take me where I was trying to go.

I wasn't the only one who noticed that I had outgrown the label. Rick Ross launched his own imprint, Maybach Music Group, in 2009. Every time Ross dropped music, the streets were on fire. He pivoted from making that raw, dope-dealer music to songs that tapped into a more elevated lifestyle and bossed-up mindset. He was able to add a layer of business mentality into his brand and his music, and it still went up in the clubs. His third studio album was the first one he did on his own label, and it has features from the best of the best: The-Dream, Wayne, Nas, and Kanye. He went crazy. Ross had learned enough about the business side of the game to know how real money was made, so even though he was doing well as a solo artist, he was ready to grow MMG and sign other people to the label. There was a lot of alignment between how Ross was shaping his career and what I was trying to do with mine. There were conversations started about me possibly joining the MMG roster. I was open to the idea because I recognized the opportunity for growth there. I'd worked with Ross since the beginning of my career. He was one of the people who taught me how to make a song. Just like everybody at Slip-N-Slide, he was family, and our bond was strong.

Neither Ross nor I was going to do a backdoor deal to get me on MMG. Ted knew I was looking at other options, and he was scrambling to figure out an alternative that would get me to stay. He had a lot on his plate. Not only was promotion for *Amazin'* still going on, but Slip-N-Slide had signed the R & B group Jagged Edge in 2009 and still hadn't released their album. Ted knew that he couldn't give me everything I wanted in a deal, but he also knew he'd be taking a loss to lose me. He proposed a joint deal for me between Slip-N-Slide and MMG. I was fine with the arrangement if it helped me become the kind of artist I wanted to be, and everyone else was on board. But Ross had a bottom line to think about, too. They tried to work it out, and I was put in the middle of business negotiations between two people I knew personally. I refused to choose sides because I loved them both, but ultimately, I didn't have to. Ross wasn't budging, and I didn't want to sign to MMG without Ted's blessing. Slip-N-Slide wasn't evolving, and I couldn't stay there, either. So I chose an option that neither of them considered for me. I chose independence.

I put off the conversation with Ted for weeks. I knew he was going through a tough time, and I hated that I had to add more bad news to his plate. It was 2011, the Jagged Edge album was finally out and not doing as well as the label wanted it to. Unfortunately, this only made me more confident about my decision. I wasn't the twentysomething girl he knew in the '90s who needed him to show her the ropes and hold her hand through the industry anymore. I knew how to make shit happen and could do it without stressing about the cost of wigs and makeup. My decision to leave the label was never about my loyalty or love for him. This was business, and I knew he would understand that. He did, but that didn't stop him from being devastated when I broke the news. Ted changed my life and gave me a career that took me further than I ever thought I would go. I made sure he knew how grateful I was for that. He is family and always will be. He could cheer me on from the sidelines, but I was my own coach now.

Leaving Slip-N-Slide at the height of my career could have very well been the end of the baddest bitch. But I was more excited than I'd been in years when I left my label. I wasn't just bossy; I was my own boss for the first time in my life. I felt strong, indestructible, and accomplished. If I didn't put out another piece of music after *Amazin'*, I would have been content.

One feature verse on "Nann" kicked off a ten-year run in the game. It wasn't always because of a high-profile relationship, or the way my ass looked in jeans. It was because I'd jumped off the porch with a mission to make music for women, and I completed that mission with every project. *XXL* named me the most consistent female rapper of all time for a reason. For the first decade of the millennium, I kept enough momentum to drop five albums. No matter how much I diversified my sound, every last one of those albums has a Trina classic on it.

On "Nann," I said I wasn't ashamed of anything I did,

and I could still stand on that. No matter what haters said to drag it through the mud, my name was solid in the industry. Even people I cut out of my life could speak to my integrity. I walked away from Slip-N-Slide on a strong foundation, and that meant more to me than any chart numbers or awards. Nothing about going independent was a downgrade or falloff. I'd come far enough to chart the rest of the path on my own in what felt like new territory.

Amazin' dropped in May 2010, and only two other female rappers released albums that year: Rah Digga dropped *Classic*, and Nicki Minaj released her debut project, *Pink Friday*. Nicki didn't limit herself to traditional hip-hop and made several pop records that were international hits. For the next few years, she was the only female MC getting consistent radio play and seeing commercial success. The days of the rap girls running in the same circles like Eve, Missy, and I did in the early 2000s were over because among her generation, Nicki was basically peerless. Not only was I proud of her individual success, but I was also proud of Young Money's growth as a label, knowing how much work Wayne put into it. The success some of his artists achieved wasn't easy for any label to accomplish.

Selling records in the 2010s was really like the Wild West. Nobody was pushing CDs from the trunk of their cars outside of parties and in barbershops anymore, unless they were bootleg copies. People were still trying to understand if it was good business to put music on the internet. Platforms like YouTube or mixtape sites like DatPiff are where people could listen to new music. If listeners liked what they heard, they could download the songs and put them on their iPods or MP3 players. Personal home computers were expensive and not as standard as they are now. To put it in context, Missy was the only person I knew who had her own computer for years. So who was going to drive numbers for hip-hop if the whole music industry was relying on internet connections? Plus, even with download numbers being recognized, your music could be bootlegged on pirating sites. We didn't know smartphones would eventually help everybody access music whenever they wanted to, or that the industry would consider streaming numbers just as much as units sold.

Thankfully, I wasn't in a position where I had to worry about selling records right away. Hitting the road, doing shows, and selling merch are the tried-and-true ways to make money as an artist. All my consistency over the years had paid off and was working in my favor. I was still in demand for shows, hosting gigs, and feature verses. Even in the absence of moving a bunch of units, I could easily pull six figures in a weekend after I went independent. I had a head start on the business model that dominates the industry now. Very few artists are commercially successful enough to sit back and live off royalties from album or single sales. Streaming numbers might do wonders on the charts, but they pay in pennies. Sponsorships from liquor or electronics companies pay for music videos instead of labels. Social media collaborations with brands pay the bills between albums and keep artists in the spotlight.

However, I didn't leave Slip-N-Slide with the intention to never make music again. If anything, I was excited about being able to approach music from a purely authentic place for the first time ever. I could revisit some of the songs I liked but that had never made it onto my albums. I could experiment with different genres and sounds and not have to defend every choice. I could work with people I'd admired for years but couldn't reach across label bureaucracy. I had so many ideas, so many old verses that people sent me, just sitting around. I wasn't pressed about being on the radio, in video countdowns, or at award shows. I was free. I just needed to figure out where to start. I was staring at an empty canvas and drawing a blank.

Ted graciously kept the Slip-N-Slide studio doors open for me to record in, but I didn't have the same team in place. None of the guys that I would have normally called to get beats or inspiration were around. Ross was gone, Plies was off doing his own thing, and Trick wasn't really making music during this time. So I called up my guy E-Class. He was the founder of Poe Boy Music Group, which was like a brother label to Slip-N-Slide. He knew everybody, and his ear was always to the streets. I told him I was working on a new project, but I still didn't know how I wanted it to feel and sound. It was like E-Class knew the call was coming. I started getting emails right away with beats and introductions to producers. Any hesitancy melted away, and just like that I was inspired again.

With my new independence, hitting the studio didn't feel like so much of a chore. Laying new tracks really felt like playtime, and whenever I finished something I liked, I couldn't wait to let my fans hear it. Being on the road constantly made this part easy because I got to see how they responded to new records in real time. I'll never forget when I had a show booked on Valentine's Day during the NBA All-Star weekend in New Orleans. I wanted to test a song called "You" about being better off without a toxic man and vowing to put myself first. The message was perfect for the occasion. But no one would have ever guessed that it was a Trina record based on the first few chords. It had a country-pop vibe. It was up-tempo and not at all what the crowd would be expecting from me, but I played it anyway. The crowd absolutely hated it. I could see them looking at me with blank stares, mad as hell, wanting me to move on to "Look Back at Me." To this day, I love "You" because I put a lot of heart into the lyrics. It didn't devastate me that fans didn't flock to it. Like every artist, I have hard-core fans that will love everything I do because it's me. But sometimes I have to be strategic when leading them toward a new vision or direction. Every project needs a story they can follow, or fans attach the material to whatever story you told them before. I'm so grateful I have a connection with my fans that persists even when we aren't on the same page.

My first few years as an independent artist were so dope because I was experimenting all the time. I didn't have to fit neatly into a box of rap, pop, trap, or any other genre. Fans and critics complain about rappers "going pop" or "switching up" like it's a bad thing, but the truth is that artists want to try different shit sometimes. There's nothing wrong with switching up if you want to try something different. Why not? When

Auto-Tune became popular in rap, a lot of people called it the death of hip-hop and R & B. But guys who normally couldn't sing layered with their own texture and tone to make melodic bops that they never would have touched otherwise. Now artists like T-Pain are beloved and recognized for how they've innovated sounds. We love every hook Future is on. Imagine if either of them fixated on how the songs would perform instead of just trying what they wanted to try. That was the wave I was on.

I needed a name for the company that I was going to operate all my business through. For years I was known as this unfiltered, in-your-face, unapologetic woman because of my lyrics and persona. I always felt like I was living the life of a real-life rock star, not afraid to take any risks or face any consequences. I've skydived multiple times just for the adrenaline rush. My fans have always flocked to that part of my personality because they're just as fearless. They're bold as hell and have never been ashamed to sing the nastiest words or talk their shit right along with me. They're rock stars, too. This is what planted the seed for Rockstarr Music Group, the umbrella company that supports my ventures and projects with other artists I sign.

I set up my own imprint in the early 2000s when I was still with Slip-N-Slide. It was called Diva Enterprises, and I signed a young artist who was really destined to be a star. I met Brianna when she was only nine years old. Her uncles had been helping her record and perform all over Miami, and as soon as I heard her, I believed in her potential. Even at that age, she had a powerful singing voice and could spit bars with clarity. She was an adorable little girl with a fiery personality. She understood her potential as an entertainer, and I signed her right off the bat. With only a few years in the game under my own belt, I took for granted how little time I had to focus on anything other than promoting my own projects. I was too busy touring, recording, and shooting to really dedicate myself to my own label. With no label and my own schedule, I could start over and give Rockstarr more of the attention it deserved. I was putting so many creative ideas into my own career; why shouldn't I set myself up to do the same thing for other artists?

Chapter 22

When French Montana and I became close, I was single and in a great space with my career. We ran in some of the same circles around Miami, but he wasn't one of my close friends. He was going through a divorce at the time, but whenever we had to interact with each other, the vibes were clearly there. I can tell when a man is interested in me, even if he isn't forthright about it. I know to fall back and wait until they lay their cards on the table and show their hand. With French, we fell into a routine of seeing each other socially more often. He wanted me to hang out at the places he was hanging, and he wanted to be wherever I was kicking it. If I was in town, I was pretty much guaranteed to see him every day. Eventually he did become someone I considered a friend, and we collaborated on music and traveled together if we had a show booked in the same city.

We went from hanging out in groups to going on dates, but French was not my man, and I was not his woman. We had a good time together, but I wasn't interested in being in a relationship with somebody that was still going through a divorce. I didn't mind spending time with him and going out, but there were still boundaries in place. He needed to handle his business, and I gave him the space to do that. The blogs didn't know all those details, though. Once people started seeing us out together, the narrative was that we were a couple. There was no appropriate way for me to clarify that French and I weren't in an exclusive relationship, or why. I just let people think what they wanted to think. Trying to clear your name in this industry is just offering more details for them to question you about. Even a few years later, when it came out that French was in a relationship with someone else, the media reported it like I had been cheated on and betrayed. That's not what happened. It certainly would have been nice to find out from his own mouth, and not the internet, that he was with someone. Please know I told him as much. But like many other things, that conversation stayed between us.

Anybody with a camera or smartphone can be a "source" for internet tabloids. The blogs can report a story and run updates on it every day, multiple times a day, as long as someone keeps feeding them the info. But the information is not always in context or the truth. I've committed to keeping my relationship details private, choosing to share my experiences and opinions in my music, not in a caption. When I'm in a relationship, I'm dedicated, but having or finding a man has never been a priority for me, because men are always around. It's hard to date and get to know people, because the moment I'm photographed sitting down for dinner with somebody, it's all over the internet. It gets blown up into a story and lives permanently online. Some of the guys that I have been reported to be in these serious relationships with over the years were actually just guys I agreed to go out with once but never had a second date with. Trust me—it *didn't* need to be news. All anybody ever needs to know about Trina and a man is that he's not going to play in my face, whether he's famous or not.

Trina the artist is an enhanced, performed version of who I am in real life. I learned early how to turn it off, and I like who I am when I do. I understand that for fans and observers, it's hard to separate those two people, which is why I don't go out of my way to clear up rumors about my personal life. Being an entertainer has always just been a job to me. The woman I am when the cameras are off is and will remain a mystery.

Chapter
23

My family has always been the center of my world. I talked to my mom every single day, and that didn't change once I started making music. She was my first line of defense in every situation. One time I called her from China, not realizing that it was the middle of the night for her, trying to figure out if it was safe for me to eat one of their dishes—like she would know. I could have just met one of the most interesting people on the planet, and the juiciest conversation of my day would still be with my mom and sister about what was going on in Miami. I never missed a beat with the day-to-day stuff, and having that kind of normalcy saved me. That's one of the biggest reasons I never left Miami except for my short stint in Denver. I hated that work caused me to miss so many important moments with my family, good or bad. Living in Miami meant I was more likely to be around to throw birthday parties, go to graduations, help make arrangements for funerals, or just kick it with my cousins and talk shit all night.

Laura is one of my best friends, and I treated my little brother, Goonkie, like he was my own kid. I bought him his first car and was just as proud as Nessa watching him walk across the stage to graduate from high school. When Laura gave birth to my niece Suga, she might as well have been the new princess of Miami. I was so obsessed with that little girl. As soon as she was old enough, I had her out with me, traveling and shopping. It wasn't enough for me to just buy stuff for Goonkie and Suga; I wanted them to know they were loved. I never wanted any of my people to feel like I was the person who flew in every once in a blue moon to throw money at their problems and then fly out again.

.... ✦ ....

One day when I was in Dallas with Kenyon, I got a call from Nessa, and she was in a frenzy. She was talking so fast it was hard to understand her, but I pieced it together: *Goonkie had been shot. I needed to get to Miami immediately.* In all my life I'd never heard that kind of panic in my mom's voice. It scared the shit out of me. I rushed to the airport, trying to call everybody I could think of to find out what was going on. I prayed during the entire flight that my baby brother would still be alive when I got to Miami. I went straight from the airport to the hospital, and I will never forget what I saw when I got to his triage room.

Goonkie had been shot in the neck and was still able to walk into the hospital on his own, but he was in bad shape. His head was so swollen that if the rest of my family hadn't been there, I wouldn't have even known it was him. I was horrified. He was conscious until the moment I got there, and then I watched him start to fade out. The doctors rushed in and took him to the operating room for surgery. It was hell sitting in that waiting room not knowing if he was going to pull through. It was hell thinking about what would happen to my mom if he didn't.

When the surgeon told us that Goonkie was going to survive, I was relieved, but I was also stunned. It's truly amazing what modern medicine can do and what the human body can handle. My brother came really close to losing his life that day and had a long road of physical recovery ahead of him. I wasn't sure how any of us would heal from the emotional trauma. Personally, I was on a warpath. I wanted to know exactly why this had happened, and I wasn't getting answers that made sense, even though a couple of my cousins were there when it happened. I tried to piece everything together: They were riding in the car. Someone started shooting. Goonkie turned around to look. He was hit. No one knew who did it.

That wasn't good enough for me.

My stepfather was almost as well-connected as Mr. Wonderful in Miami. When Mike Tyson was in town, he hung out with Willie on Fifteenth Avenue. That's how well respected he was. My brother grew up with the same protection Laura and I had. This wasn't supposed to happen to him. Was he targeted? Did I need to be worried about the rest of my family? When he was finally healed enough to tell me what happened, it filled in some of the holes in what other people had said. He was in the wrong place at the wrong time and became a victim of random violence. That didn't make me feel any better. I wanted to protect my family, but life is so unpredictable, and I couldn't be there all the time. No amount of money or power can guarantee anyone's safety 24/7. All I could do was move him in with me in Denver while he got better, and my nerves settled. At last, he was safe for now.

Five years later, on April 23, 2013, Nessa called me at nine in the morning. I was still in bed at my condo in Aventura, but I was thankful for the wake-up call because I was supposed to do a video shoot with French and The Weeknd later that day.

"Are you sleeping?" That's all she asked me, but I could tell something wasn't right. Her voice was hiding something else.

"I'm up. What's wrong?"

Silence. Whatever it was, she didn't want to speak the words. "Your little brother is dead." I placed the unsteadiness in her voice. She sounded the same way when she called to tell me he had been shot.

I needed to make sure I heard her correctly. I thought she'd said my brother was dead, but maybe I was still asleep, and this was a bad dream. "What?"

"He's gone."

I was up and pacing the floor. I made it to my balcony, and when I looked over the railing, I thought I would fall over the ledge as the weight of what I'd just heard sank in. I needed to do something. I needed get out of there.

My body went into autopilot, throwing on clothes and grabbing keys so that I could go find my brother. I hopped into the car and sped toward Nessa's house. Goonkie was killed right around the corner from her home. I turned onto the block, saw all the police tape and cars, and went berserk. I sped up instead of slowing down and blew right past the first barricade. Not knowing if I was a threat, some of the officers pulled out their guns, ready to shoot at my car. I heard someone screaming, "Stop! That's Trina! That's his sister!" I finally stopped the car and hopped out but forgot to put it in park. One of the officers reached in to grab the wheel and caught it. I was screaming at everybody, asking where my brother was and what happened to him. There was no ambulance or sense of urgency on the scene, and that pissed me off even more. Why wasn't anyone trying to treat him?! There was no ambulance because there was nothing a hospital could have done for him. The coroner was already there. There was no hope for a surgery or recovery this time. My little brother was really gone. The man who had taken him from us was already in the back of one of the squad cars, and it took several officers to keep me from him.

For the next few weeks and months, I went completely numb and dark. I hadn't felt this low since Hollywood passed, but this time it was worse because Goonkie was my blood, my baby. Not only was I hurting, but I had to watch my mother—the strongest woman I knew—bury her child. She was completely devastated, and I was worried that she blamed herself for what happened. She'd said to me in a daze, "No matter how much you try to protect your kids, teach them to be careful, and tell them not to have guns on them and to only use them if they have to protect themselves and to not bother anybody, they still get taken out by one." She sounded so defeated, like she had let my brother down, and that broke my heart even more. None of us could have prevented Gonk from being killed, just like none of us could have prevented the first time he was shot. My little brother was not perfect, but he wasn't reckless, either. He was killed by someone he knew, in his neighborhood, right around the corner from his own mother's house, after trying to de-escalate a situation. It made me sick to my stomach thinking about it.

Losing my brother completely changed my life. It made me so much more anxious and paranoid. The best decision I made during that time was to not be on social media while my family mourned my brother. I stepped back from as much work as I could in an effort to deal with my grief and support my family through theirs. It wasn't until six months later, when we were throwing a party on his birthday to celebrate his life, that I posted about it on social media. That's when I realized how much media coverage there was of his death. I saw the hundreds of comments offering prayers and sending condolences to me and my family. None of their words could do anything to make the loss less painful, but it was a reminder that not every piece of the internet was negative or filled with hate.

Chapter
24

Mona Scott-Young changed the game when she created *Love & Hip Hop* in 2011. She understood how invested the fans were in the real lives and stories behind hip-hop artists, and she used her music-industry connections to create this huge franchise. It opened doors for so many artists, their teams, and their families to expand their businesses and get a bigger bag. For a long time, it was the reality franchise that consistently pulled in the highest number of viewers. It was the inspiration for a lot of similar series. Mona kept Missy as her only management client and fully committed to being a TV executive. I had so much respect for her success and hustle. She really created a phenomenon. But when she first approached me about joining the cast to do a version in Miami, I said, "Hell, no."

I had seen episodes of *Love & Hip Hop* based in the other cities—Hollywood, Atlanta, and New York—and it didn't look like anything I wanted to be part of. There was too much focus on people's relationship drama, there were a lot of messy arguments, and actual fights broke out way too often. I couldn't imagine myself in any situation where sitting down to have a conversation with somebody ends with wigs getting yanked off people's heads. Somebody throwing a drink in my face? Absolutely not. I wear contact lenses and could just imagine myself flying into a literal blind rage. None of it seemed professional or "safe" for anybody involved. It wasn't a good look to me, and it wasn't how I wanted to present myself to fans or the general public. I didn't care about the money, the opportunities it could bring, or how well I knew Mona. For years, my answer was no.

I wasn't a complete stranger to reality TV; I just felt like there was a right way to do it. When La La and Melo got married, they documented all the planning, the buildup to the wedding, and the ceremony for a show on VH1. It did so well that she ended up getting a spin-off that followed her family after they left Denver and got settled in New York. The show focused on her career, being a mom, and how the rest of her friends and family fit into all that. I filmed a few episodes with her as a guest, and it was dope to see how she worked with the team to figure out what to share and if it made sense. She didn't have to deal with other entertainers or athletes that she didn't know as part of the cast, which was the recipe for chaos on other shows. Having control over the storyline, who was involved, and whatever the final output looked like was the most important thing for me. If I could do reality like that, maybe it wouldn't be so bad.

Years before Mona asked me about *Love & Hip Hop*, a friend of mine got me a meeting with Tracey Edmonds, the amazing television producer behind the *Soul Food* series and the limited reality series documenting Lil' Kim's time before she turned herself in to prison. I took a meeting with her in Los Angeles, and she said she was willing to produce a fun, light-hearted show about me, my family, and my life in Miami. We wanted to play on the theme of *Glamorest Life* but in a down-to-earth, humorous way. She got a pilot green-lit for us and flew into Miami to shoot it.

The entire cast had been handpicked by me, including my cousin Joy and a much younger cousin that I hadn't known as long. Bobby is my cousin on my biological father's side, so he was a stranger to me for a good chunk of his life. He literally made his way through the crowd at one of my shows, yelling about us being cousins, and I haven't been able to get rid of him since then. He was made to be on TV because everything about his personality is over-the-top and larger than life. I thought it would be dope to have him on the show because I had reconnected with my biological father for the first time in my life during this time, and if I was going to address any of that on the show, Bobby would be a great point of reference. Laura and some of my other friends were going to round it out as part of a rotating cast.

When I saw the first cut of the sizzle reel, I absolutely hated it. It didn't accurately represent me or a glamorous lifestyle at all. It looked more like a circus. The outfits weren't fitting, the glam was not glamming, and the vibes were not vibing. It was the first time most of my friends and family had ever done television. They were so awkward on camera and didn't bring the energy you need for good TV. The show was my idea, not theirs, and their indifference came across onscreen. Once something is recorded, it lives forever, and I didn't want any of us to be immortalized like that. I was so hurt and disappointed, because I love Tracey and I would have loved to make a show with her. But I wanted to pull the plug on it immediately. I wasn't ready yet. The reality train would have to go on without me for a little bit longer.

The decision to finally join *Love & Hip Hop: Miami* was bigger than me. Everything had changed—the music game, the journalism industry, marketing strategies, and the definition of celebrity—except TV. Reality television was only getting more popular in 2016, even if it was ratchet. Social media was an invaluable tool to accelerate the growth. Storylines were teased online and then fleshed out on the show. *Love & Hip Hop*, specifically, was really helping new artists grow their audiences and break into the industry. I was passionate about Rockstarr Music Group and realized the show might be the best way for me to help my artists get the exposure they needed. I had other people around me who could benefit from that bag, too. I'd heard that Trick wasn't really busy with any big projects at the time. My cousin Joy, who had married Trick years earlier, was ready to work. My crazy-ass cousin

Bobby was still wild, but he also wanted to do music. It was a business opportunity that would help so many people other than me, and that's all I cared about. OG hip-hop fans and artists used to think being on reality television was something that made you soft or less serious as an artist. But at the end of the day, most of the cast members on all these shows are working just as hard as everybody else. That's the side of my career I wanted to show, and that's what finally brought me to the table.

Even Missy was surprised when I first told her I was going to do it. She didn't think it was a good idea, because she knows my personality. I have a long fuse, but once I reach my wits' end, all bets are off. She's seen it with her own eyes. She didn't want me on national TV blacking out and popping off. I was quick to tell her that I had no plans of moving like some of the people she saw on other episodes of the show in other cities. I had a long conversation with Mona to make sure we avoided that. The first thing we agreed on was that no one was going to be throwing any drinks or punches at me. We couldn't even play like that. I was also up-front about not wanting to focus on my personal, romantic relationships. I had been in enough high-profile situations to know that too much exposure on your relationship ultimately damages it. Love is complicated enough on its own, between individuals. You never know why two people are in love, what their history is, or what they're struggling with. You damn sure can't decide whether it's right for them, so inviting in all the unnecessary opinions that everyone seems to have is pointless. In that arena, a private life is a happier life. Everything going on with my crew, my music, and the label was more than enough drama to give viewers a good show. Mona and the rest of the team respected those wishes, and we moved on from there. Missy still threatened to call Mona and pull the plug if she saw anything crazy.

Knowing what could go wrong with reality TV, I considered the risks and did everything in my power to minimize a repeat of my first show. Because *Love & Hip Hop* is attached to a major cable network, there is more money for better glam, so I don't worry about my people looking their best. There are a lot of different personalities on the show, and their interactions can get messy. So I put in my contract that I control my set, who I film scenes with, and when. My comfort and safety are always the priority. At the end of the day, if you're not the one shooting, producing, writing, and editing the show, you don't have full control over how you're represented or what ends up in an episode when it airs. Even with my contract and other precautions that I've taken, I still sometimes see final scene cuts that I feel misrepresent my opinions and words. A big chunk of what I said might be edited out, and then the whole context is different. That's just the way it goes, and it's still a struggle for me to pick my battles about what to let slide and when to put my foot down. This is also why I don't get too invested in the viewers' reactions and the online commentary, because I know they're only getting bits and pieces of situations that are being aired. If I'm bickering with Trick or Bobby onscreen, know that there are so many more conversations that are going to happen about it offscreen, on the phone, in our personal text messages, and at each other's houses. It takes a lot for me to want to open up to the public about anything. So having to navigate difficult situations on a national platform is really hard. There are definitely scenes on *Love & Hip Hop* that I wish I could change because I was super pissed, got really out of character, and didn't show up as my best self. But I don't regret going on the show, because it has helped the people I wanted to help. And at the end of the day, I will never feel bad about showing people what's real.

Chapter 25

When I started Rockstarr Music Group in 2011, the plan was never to be the next Berry Gordy or take over the whole music industry. I also wasn't trying to lock artists down and control their whole life. All I wanted to do was offer other people their one shot and run my own business. For a long time, I didn't have a traditional manager. Instead, I had a handpicked team put in position to hold me down and support RMG. I cleared the roster when I went independent, and everything was on me to handle. I needed someone to help with the day-to-day stuff, someone else to handle touring and logistics, and a mediator for any business that was coming in. It was on me to make final decisions, keep up with progress, and make sure everybody got paid, even if it was out of my own pocket. With my personal energy and my funds on the line, I had to work at my own pace, in an environment I was most comfortable in. I relied on the people I already knew. I could always count on people like Redd, C.O., and KD (someone who went from making flyers for me to promoting hosting gigs and overseeing all of my partnerships). I knew I could trust all of them to have my back and get the job done. We had been in business together long enough for them to understand how the industry works.

I love bringing people new opportunities, but as they say, the road to hell is paved with good intentions. You can think you know someone and have the best hopes for their success, and they can still let you down. The truth is that some people only see what you can do for them and don't have a problem biting the hand that feeds them. There was one guy who had worked for Slip-N-Slide for years. He'd touched every one of my albums since *Diamond Princess*. He was able to soak up a lot of game over the years and had a lot of good ideas. When the label hit a rough patch, he was trying to figure out his next move just like everybody else. He was one of the people I welcomed onto my team when I was independent. He had dreams of doing bigger things in the industry as a manager and executive, and I saw that for him because I knew he was smart. I agreed to let him be my manager, a move that was supposed to help both of our careers. My team was hustling and making shit happen, but maintaining my brand and trying to build a whole business was not a cheap operation. I had already put out a bunch of mixtapes, but I had more music recorded, and I wanted to package and release it the right way. I had to be intentional about my projects if I wanted to build a platform big enough to support my signed artists. The bottom line was that we needed an investment, one bigger than I could have gotten from Slip-N-Slide. I didn't necessarily need a record deal, but my company did. I was willing to go back in-house if the terms were what I needed them to be, so my new manager and I started shopping around for a deal that would benefit the entire imprint. In a decision I still regret to this day, we signed with Penalty Entertainment in 2015. My goal was to drop my album the following year. I had no clue that it would be another four years of delays and pushbacks before it came out.

Everything that could have slowed down my last album release happened. When I first signed with them, Penalty had just restructured in a huge partnership with Sony RED, and I wasn't the only artist that they brought on that year. They were still figuring out who they were prioritizing with resources and energy. Then about a year or so after that, RED was merged under another Sony entity called The Orchard. While the huge label machine was spinning its wheels, I felt like RMG got lost in the shuffle and fell to the bottom of the totem pole. I kept recording and making songs so that the album would feel fresh when it dropped, but we also had to jump through endless hoops to get sample and feature clearances. It was wild how quickly the whole situation started to feel even more stifling than my last deal. This album had taken years to make. It was like a baby that I had raised and prayed for. After all the waiting and making changes, I felt like I finally had a body of work that represented who I was as a woman and as an artist.

The One came out just over twenty years after I got in the game, and it was supposed to be special. It deserved time and attention that it didn't receive. I learned that the person I trusted to partner with me in this phase of my career used funds from our advance for his other endeavors. He insists that he upheld his contractual obligations, but the money was gone. This left me with nothing to put toward videos or promo. The album was literally removed from streaming platforms because some of the producers who worked on it hadn't been paid. I was embarrassed and pissed. There was no excuse for dropping the ball to this magnitude, and my manager didn't even try to offer one. He went ghost on me after causing one of the biggest letdowns of my career, and he stayed ghost as I experienced one of the biggest heartbreaks and darkest times of my life.

Chapter 26

On any other Thanksgiving, I would have been working and missing out on family dinner. I didn't feel like it in 2015, and I decided to go home instead. I went straight to Nessa's from the airport, expecting to find her in the kitchen, getting a meal ready for the holiday. She was home, but she wasn't cooking. She looked tired, and she was obviously in pain. I took her to the hospital the same day. I was relieved when the doctor diagnosed her with kidney stones. I didn't want her in any pain, but at least they knew what was causing the issue and could treat it. She was scheduled for surgery to remove the stones, and that's when her prognosis went from bad to worse. Doctors removed all of her kidney stones and discovered cancer.

Her diagnosis came as a huge blow to my family. Cancer had already claimed the life of my aunt Sheila. Nessa was really involved in taking care of her sister, so we had a front-row seat to the damage it can do. I was dreading seeing my mother, my best friend, in that condition. But I tried to push my feelings aside to be there for her. I took a break from touring and doing shows to be home with her. Her comfort and health became the most important things in my life. Eventually, I had to get back to work, and my sister, Laura, stayed by her side. The cancer spread slowly, over the course of several years. One day when I talked to her on the phone, she was so sick that she didn't even sound like herself. She was superwoman to me, but in that moment, she sounded so weak and fragile. I knew that her battle was almost done. It just ripped my heart out of my chest. She was the literal center of my world, and in that moment, I wanted nothing more than for her to know it. I went to the studio and recorded "Mama" as a tribute to her, this time featuring Kelly Price. I made sure it stayed on the album, and I'm so glad I laid the track while she was still here and able to listen to it. My album came out in June, and my mother transitioned on September 3, 2019.

Even though I knew it was coming, even though I'd held my mom's hand through so much of her cancer battle, and got to tell her how much I loved her, I still wasn't emotionally ready for when she passed away. I couldn't prepare for her death, because I couldn't even imagine what the world would be like without her until she was already gone. Nessa was larger than life to me and everybody who knew her because she did so much for her family and her community. For my entire life, she was my rock. She was the foundation that kept me stable, whether I was standing tall or crumbling down. There were so many moments that were so tough that her strength was the only thing that got me through. There was nothing I didn't trust her with, nothing I couldn't talk to her about, and nothing I wouldn't have done for her. When I had to face the reality that she wasn't here anymore, it was like the ground had been pulled from underneath me. It was like I was free-falling with no parachute and nothing to grab on to. There were some days when the grief was so strong it felt like I couldn't breathe. It's the kind of pain I wouldn't wish on anybody.

When Hollywood passed away, I remember being surrounded by my mom, my sister, and my aunts. We would all gather around at my mom's house or her hair salon, and people knew that they could find me there in those first few days after it happened. These were the women I respected the most and considered to be top tier. A lot of people were coming by to see me. I was so checked out that I barely remember their faces or who they were. But the memory that has remained etched in my brain from that difficult time is one of my aunts telling every friend who stopped by the same thing. I heard her say it over and over again, and she was so adamant about it: "Don't come around here with that pity party. Don't come around here with that. Anything that is going to bring her down or make her feel worse, don't bring it around here." I didn't really understand what she meant at the time. I thought she just didn't want to see me cry. When Nessa passed away, I think I finally got it. When you are experiencing a loss on that level, there's nothing anyone can do to make you feel better or worse. All they can do is help make sure you have the space to deal with it. That's why so many people bring food, clean up, or donate things in a time of loss. It's relieving the burdens in the physical world because there is nothing that can be done about those emotional wounds. My aunt was telling my friends to make themselves useful instead of offering sympathies.

We made sure Nessa's homegoing was a full-on bash. She was the "hostess with the mostest" during her time on Earth, so we threw her a celebration of life that was just as fun and energetic. We filled the venue with decorations and balloons in her favorite color, orange. We had a live band and dancers to keep everyone on their feet and to recognize my mom's dance abilities. We had the rest of our lives to mourn and grieve her. On the day of her service, we partied.

There was a void left in my life that was impossible to fill when Nessa was gone, and I had to figure out how to get up and keep going. The death of a loved one is such a humbling experience because you are dealing with this massive, life-changing event, and the world just keeps moving and going on. There are still thousands of cars on the highway and thousands of planes in the sky filled with people who don't have a clue what you're going through. You can be up all night on a Tuesday, rolling around on the floor and crying because of the grief . . . and the next morning the sun will still come up, and it will still be Wednesday, and you still have to make sure you move your car so it doesn't get towed, or put your trash out so it can get picked up. You might need three days or three weeks to get control of your feelings, but during that time, life is still going on. In your moment of loss, nothing stops. And that time always comes after all of the arrangements have been made and handled, and all the hoopla of funerals or celebrations of life dies down, when people stop coming by and the calls get less frequent. They go back to living their life and you're still living in the emotional mess that has been left behind. Your person is still gone. Nothing can change or fix that. You just have to keep waking up and figuring out how to make it through each day, day by day. If you're lucky, the people around you can help make that part a little easier, but the emotional impact is always there. This is what it was like for me in the aftermath of Nessa's passing. It's still like that. I sometimes still cry just thinking about how much I miss my mom. There is no such thing as "feeling better" about it. I've learned to deal with and live with that pain. I had to get up and go to work just a couple of weeks later because the cameras were back on. Every day, I put one foot in front of the other and kept pushing.

After losing my first love, then my brother, then my mom, I really didn't think I could handle another loss. I didn't think the universe would be cruel enough to test my strength after everything I'd been through, but it did on July 20, 2022. That's the night my niece, Baby Suga, was shot and killed. Her name and those words, together in the same sentence, will never sit right in my spirit. But that's what happened.

My niece was only seventeen years old when she died, and she was one of my favorite people. I treated her like my own daughter. When I moved to Denver with Kenyon, she and Laura moved into my place in Miami. When I moved back, I loved spending time with her. She was so gorgeous and bright. Up until her death, she still traveled with me whenever I could bring her along, and I spoiled her all the time. It was the summer before her senior year of high school when she was struck by a stray bullet.

It happened in Liberty City, of all places, right outside the Beans. That made it worse. The place responsible for making me who I am took away the person who was most precious to me. Suga didn't deserve what happened to her; she didn't cause what happened to her; she didn't ask for what happened to her. Suga was just a kid with her whole life ahead of her, and someone took it all away in an instant. What I felt, and what my family felt, was more than just grief. I was angry. *What the fuck is going on in the world that something like this could even happen?*

If there is anything that can challenge your faith and make you question everything you believe in, it's death, especially when it's senseless and unexpected. Depending on your mental and emotional state, death can damn near make you stop believing in anything at all. I've had pretty much my entire life to think about it. At first, I accepted that it was part of some cycle of life or plan that was bigger than me, and that's why I couldn't understand it. When my mom passed, it was a process that I watched happen over time. It was awful, but it made sense. There was no rhyme or reason for Suga being gunned down in the street. It was completely random and meaningless, and that feels like the real truth of death.

Is there any mystery to it at all? Whether it's from illness, tragedy, or anything else, what meaning does death have when it can be anyone's time at any moment? You can be in the club, taking a bath, driving, watching TV, sleeping in your bed, or walking your dog, and boom. When someone dies, we talk about it being their "time," because the timing is one of the things we can never know. Death scares us, so we avoid thinking about it and keep living until it strikes again. None of us knows when it will be our time, but all of us will have our turn. It's a card that we were dealt the moment we were born. It doesn't matter who you are or what you've done. You can be dirt-poor or have all the money in the world. It doesn't matter how big your house is, what kind of car you drive, how much your jewelry costs, or how many designer labels you wear. You can be big or small, be drop-dead gorgeous, have fake boobs and a BBL, or be all natural. It doesn't matter if you eat pork or have been vegan for your entire life.

It doesn't matter how many books I write, how many songs I record, how many stages I perform on, how many awards I win, or how many lives I change. One day it's going to be me. One day it's going to be a person who hasn't done a fraction of what I've done. One day it's going to be someone I can't stand. One day it's going to be someone else I love. I've gotten to a point where I see nothing divine or special about death. I no longer get caught up in my head trying to figure out how it fits into God's plan. What is the point when none of us can change it or make sense of it?

To this day, I still haven't heard a single word that is actually comforting about my niece's passing. When Suga died, I was so disgusted with the world that I didn't want to hear from anybody. If anyone thought it was possible to comfort me, they were delusional. I wanted everybody out of my face. A friend of mine is a pastor, and he called to offer prayers and some spiritual counseling. None of it resonated with me. He was reciting words from a book, and they didn't make sense to me in the face of what I was dealing with. We're taught to say a lot of things to people who are grieving to be polite, and none of them are useful. If I respond to any of these questions honestly, *I'm* not being polite:

Are you okay? Of course I'm not.

How do you feel? I feel awful. I'm depressed. I haven't slept. I have a thousand things to do, and I don't want to talk about how I feel.

I'm sorry about your loss. You're not sorrier than I am.

I know people mean well, but that doesn't make it less cringey. Now imagine navigating those conversations with strangers who don't always respect your privacy or boundaries. Being a public figure has added an entirely new layer to my grief. I noticed it a lot after my mom passed because I went back to work so soon afterward. It would take so much energy to get up, get dressed, and be present anywhere in decent spirits. Then I would arrive, be in the middle of doing my thing, and someone would approach me with good intentions to congratulate or compliment me. That would make me feel proud that I was still showing up to live my life. Then, right before they'd say their goodbyes, they would add, *I'm sorry about your mom.* They would bring to the front of my mind the one thing I didn't want to think about. They would carry on feeling good about themselves while I'd struggle to hold back tears. It would piss me off so bad. No two people are going to feel the same way when they're grieving, but it felt like I was tending a wound that never stopped hurting. People would throw salt in it even when they didn't mean to. I had to learn how to mentally detach from those experiences and not take them personally so that it wouldn't throw me into misery and chaos.

.... ✦ ....

When I was a little girl spending time at my grandma's house, she used to always tell me, "You are very spoiled. But outside of this gate where you're safe with me, the world is full of lions and tigers and bears. And when you grow up and get out there, they are going to be ready to eat your ass alive." I was used to Caribbean mamas, aunties, and grandmas saying the most dramatic things to try to scare kids into acting right. I thought that's what she was doing because I took it literally. There weren't any lions, tigers, or bears roaming around Liberty City, so I never paid it any mind. I couldn't appreciate what she was really trying to tell me about life until I got older. The world is full of scary shit waiting to take your joy, your confidence, or even your life. Sometimes it's people close to you that betray you. Sometimes you cross paths with complete strangers who turn your world upside down. Sometimes it's not a person at all. Sometimes your own demons and circumstances can make life harder for you. If you keep living, you are going to experience heartbreak, tragedy, loss, sickness, grief, and darkness. You can't avoid them. That's just the reality of life. That's what my grandmother was talking about, and I've accepted that. The lions and tigers and bears never go away, but I know to expect them now. And I definitely know better than to ever lie down and let them eat me alive.

Chapter 27

When *Da Baddest Bitch* came out, momentum was full force. The label was happy, the critics were watching and excited about it, and the music industry was opening even more doors for me. In a matter of months, I went from doing shows on local and regional stages to national ones. The year 2001 was the first-ever BET Awards ceremony in Las Vegas, and I was nominated for Best Female Hip-Hop Artist. The two things about that day I'll never forget are how hot it was and how much I hated the spikey flips they put in my hair.

It was similar to Missy's hair in her "Get Ur Freak On" video, but it looked ridiculous on me. The stylist kept trying to convince me that the hairdo went perfectly with the custom denim outfit I had on. The BET Awards were a major televised event, and it was one of the first times I had worked with a styling team that didn't include my mom doing my hair. I decided to go along with their creative vision for my look. I was a new artist attending one of my first major award shows. I didn't want to cause a scene or have people thinking I was hard to work with. When I hit the red carpet hours later, I saw variations of the same hairstyle on several other women. Apparently it was trendy, and that made me hate it even more. But I wasn't going to let a bad hair day ruin my night.

Once we got inside the Paris hotel, they ushered me to my assigned seat, and it sank in that I was in the same room as Patti LaBelle, Luther Vandross, Whitney Houston, and Mary J. Blige. Sitting among such greatness was a lot to take in. My life had done a complete one-eighty from giving lap dances three years prior. Somehow it all made sense, though. I'd worked hard on my album, and this wasn't a bad payoff. Every time I go to an award show, I let myself soak in that gratitude.

I was nominated for Best Female Hip-Hop Artist alongside Lil' Kim and Da Brat (two women that I had looked up to for years) and Missy and Eve (two women I could honestly call friends). I was in my seat feeling like more of a fan than an artist when they listed out the nominees. The winner was Eve. I hopped out of my seat to clap and cheer just as loud as everybody else. I was so proud and happy for my girl because she deserved it. We partied all night with some of the most talented people in the industry to celebrate.

The next year, 2002, I was nominated in the same category for *Diamond Princess*. I knew I wasn't going to win, because Missy was also in the category, and she was on fire. She was the reason I was also a Video-of-the-Year nominee, thanks to "One Minute Man." I was surprised we didn't take that one home, but her win of Best Female Hip-Hop Artist was a win for me, too. In 2003, 2006, and 2008, we were both nominated for that award, and Missy won the trophy for both of us every time. I was hopeful about my chances in 2009, when there were only two other nominees and both of them were brand-new to the industry. I didn't win that year, either, which admittedly stung because I was already four albums and almost a decade in. I addressed it on *Amazin'* and kept it moving. When I was nominated in 2010, 2012, and 2015, Nicki took the awards home. She was Wayne's artist and the breath of fresh air the industry needed. How could I be mad about that?

For years, haters tried to discredit my work and impact by bringing up my lack of awards. But I didn't get into this game for the accolades. I saw an opportunity to boss up and be successful, and I took it and ran with it. I've spent my entire career putting the best parts of my personality, my city, and my attitude on display. I was able to take care of my mom, my siblings, my nieces and nephews, and the rest of my family. I traveled the world. Every time I was nominated, I got to sit in a room with my idols, wearing designer clothes, and feeling like a million bucks in celebration of the records and albums I put out that year. People always clapped at the mention of my name. I was blessed, and I had everything I came into the game to get.

I have a network of people that are brilliant and will always keep it real with me. I came up in this industry and spent the best years of my life with one of the most iconic record labels out of the South. I spent years with one of the greatest rappers alive, and he's still someone I can call just to chop it up with. My friends are legends and visionaries. Being genuine and keeping genuine people around has unlocked so many doors for me. I couldn't ask for much more than that.

I found out that the BET Hip Hop Awards was bestowing me with their highest honor—the I Am Hip Hop Award—in 2022. I hadn't dropped any projects and was dealing with so much personal grief that I could barely absorb what was happening. I accepted the award in Atlanta surrounded by my team and my Slip-N-Slide family. I cried because my brother, my mom, and my niece weren't there to see it. It still meant the world to me, though. After years of leaving the main awards empty-handed, I was given my flowers—not for a song or an album, but for all of it: for two decades of hard work and experimentation, for being a blueprint for so many other women.

It was a reminder that I can keep going at my own pace. I know that I've done enough. I've given enough of myself to deserve the accolades and the respect. That's what I stand on and sleep well at night knowing. I've made six studio hip-hop albums. The only other female rapper with that many is Missy. I am so proud of that. I don't have anything left to prove, because I know I've done my job. I leave it to the critics and the fans to put the pieces together about what my career has meant for the industry and other women in hip-hop, because that's their job.

Truth be told, when people ask me about my legacy or impact in the industry, I'm sometimes at a loss for words. I don't always know when the debates are happening about who has the best catalog or influence. I sometimes don't even know when I'm trending on Twitter. When I think about my career, I know I'm successful because it's been twenty-five years, and I can still get a crowd active. When girls come up to me and tell me how my music inspired them, I know I did exactly what I set out to do when I first started.

One of the things the music and entertainment industries have in common with the streets is how easy it is to get caught up in a toxic cycle. There is always another check, another award, another milestone dangled in front of you, and you're supposed to chase them no matter the cost. You're expected to change your sound, your appearance, your schedule, your location, your accent, and even your opinions every time the trends change. You have these phones that are constantly reinforcing what everybody else thinks of you, what you should be doing, and what you did wrong. You end up on this hamster wheel that never stops, and if you run for long enough, you'll forget what you were chasing in the first place. It's a lot of smoke and mirrors, and you can definitely get lost in it.

When I look back on my life and think about all the ways it might have turned out—I could have been in the car with Hollywood that night; I could have sold that house to that family and become a real estate mogul; I could have gotten caught up in the life at the strip club and lost myself; I could have stayed with Atlantic Records and sold 100 million more records than I did—there are a lot of *couldas* and *shouldas*. But I fully believe I'm right where I'm supposed to be.

The same year I won the I Am Hip Hop Award, I held my first Trina Day in Liberty City. It was a community-based event for kids and families to come together, have fun, and get free backpacks and school supplies. I couldn't let what happened to my niece turn me away from giving back to the community that gave so much to me. The mayor of Miami showed up to decree May 14 "Trina Day" and present me with a key to the city. I know that my grandparents, who left their island to literally build a life in Miami, would have been so proud.

In 2022, I renewed my real estate license for the first time in years. I've been investing in real estate since the moment I made enough money to. What I love more than the passive income is the process of deciding remodel details, choosing the décor for the staging, and the entrepreneurial mind it forces me to use. The little girl who wanted to be an architect is still in there somewhere. I also want to be a resource to others aspiring to break into the market and level up. Creating even more events and experiences in Miami, on land I own, is always a goal for me. The achievements of my lifetime are far from over.

Epilogue

······· ◆ ·······

In 2023, I hosted my first-ever Rockstarr Music Festival, and I made sure the lineup was full of mostly female artists. I still think women are the most interesting entertainers in this game. They always come in with a bang, dropping that record everybody loves. You hear it in the club, and the whole room goes up. Their presence is stronger than everybody else's and they possess that "thing" that makes you want to pay attention to them. There is so much versatility and range from the girls now. They all have different sounds and styles, and I firmly believe there is a lane for everybody—for the girls that like to sing as much as they rap, for the girls that make songs about their favorite cartoon characters, for the girls that twerk on the headlights and have their homegirls from the hood in every single video. I have heard some songs that are so ratchet that I can't help but burst out laughing. I've heard others where I couldn't believe the person I saw on IG was the same girl in the booth. We went from years of having one or two girls out at a time to me not even being able to keep up with all the girls rapping. They're taking hip-hop to its new heights.

I see myself in so many of these girls today, and it's not because they're talking nasty and calling themselves bad bitches. It's because I remember being young in this industry and knowing that I had to make choices that were going to decide my whole future. There was so much on the line, and the opportunity was so big. I had to either sink or swim. I had goals to hit, and the stakes were real. I know there are girls trying to rap who have to make it work or they're going back to clocking in at somebody's nine-to-five or trying to make their hair business or boutique pop off. They have to make it work or they're back to being bottle girls, bartenders, or dancers. They have to make it work or they're going to be stuck in an abusive, toxic relationship. They have to make it work or they'll be lost.

When these girls tell me my music has been a blueprint or an inspiration for them, I get flashbacks to sneaking out of the back of the store to watch the women in the Uncle Luke video and eavesdropping on the ladies in my mom's shop when I was supposed to stay out of grown folks' conversations. I see the silly things young people take seriously these days, but you never know how those random memories can shape you and follow you into adulthood.

━━━ ◆ ━━━

Keenya was a friend of mine from Miami growing up. She was another baddie in the city, and we always ran in similar circles. She used to get her hair done at my mom's shop, and we saw each other at parties and clubs as we got older. She had a beautiful baby girl named Caresha, who became my goddaughter. Caresha was only four years old when I started rapping, but whenever I could, I made sure I spent time with her. One year, I took her to the county fair with a security detail. I wanted it to be a normal experience, but she noticed the people trying to wave and say hello to me. She thought it was so cool that her godmom was a celebrity, and she was smiling back at them like she was, too.

Caresha was always confident and self-assured. When she got older, she was gorgeous, fashionable, and popping on social media. She was becoming an It Girl just like her godmom, even though she still had to navigate motherhood and life in some rough parts of Miami. I was surprised when she started rapping with her friend JT because I didn't think she'd go the music route, but they took it seriously. They called themselves City Girls and did shows around Miami. When one of their songs went viral and they signed to Quality Control, I was so happy for them and even happier that they had each other to navigate the industry with.

Neither Keenya nor I would have turned my curse-filled songs on to set a good example for Caresha when she was a little girl. Not many parents would. But she still learned how to make her confidence work for her. She was able to completely change her and Keenya's life because City Girls became one of the most successful hip-hop groups. She was in the same position I was, having to sink or swim, and she had a blueprint for how to make it work. That's the impact I'm most grateful to have on any woman's life.

There are so many different paths for women to take in the industry, but it's not complete freedom. People see pretty pictures and hear confident lyrics, and they don't consider how hard it is out here for these girls. They are criticized so heavily, picked apart for what they look like, held to a different lyrical standard, and constantly put in competition with other women. The commentary is nonstop, and that can be such a huge block to creativity. It's so easy for strangers to make a mockery of the art these women put their heart and passion into. Not to mention there are plenty of shady, trifling men waiting for a chance to take advantage of them. I was blessed to step into the industry with a group of guys who always had my back, but I know a lot of women don't have that.

My advice to all the women in the industry is to do your thing to the fullest. Talk your shit. Feel comfortable in your skin. I'm not ever going to bend over to take a picture with my hand in my butt crack. But if it works for you, you should do it. If you want to be raunchy and ratchet as hell and shake your ass, you should do it. What's the problem? It might not work for this crew, and it might not be the right cup of tea for that crew, but *somebody* is going to love it. You don't need to seek validation from anyone else. Do what you want to do, not what everybody thinks you should be doing. Remember who you are, put yourself first, and go for it. Lean into the alter ego because you're going to need one when you're putting yourself out there for the public to consume you. Have fun with it and know that you can always change your mind. You are making songs, videos, and TikToks. This is not a presidential election. Yes, everything lives on the internet forever, but you are always in control of the tone you set. You can rebrand, pivot, or stop at any time. Don't take yourself too seriously or succumb to the pressure to stay the same. As long as you're confident and willing to stand ten toes down on what you decide to do, there will still be a platform for you to put it out on and make a check.

Rockstarr Music Festival is one of those platforms. I uplift and support the women coming in the game behind me. I've already earned my respect, so I don't need younger artists to bow down at my feet or kiss my ass in order for me to show them love or collaborate with them. I'm not trying to be the deciding factor on who the best female rapper is, if this girl is trying to sound like someone else, if she's classy or hood enough, or if her brand is exactly where it needs to be. These are artists. They don't need my stamp of approval to keep doing their thing, but I'm happy to point them in the right direction.

It's not enough to get paid for a feature or give somebody a quick shout-out in an interview. Creating opportunities for them to get better and grow is just as important. I remember watching Eve and Missy win their Grammys and knowing it was so special because Lauryn Hill was the only other woman in the game who had done it. It felt so monumental. Cardi B is a global superstar and the first female solo artist to win a Best Rap Album Grammy. Now we don't have to wait years to see women nominated in top categories. The girls are always exceptional, but we're not exceptions anymore.

.... ◆ ....

For me, being the baddest was never just about the physical beauty, the money, the status symbols, or perfection. I've been fine all of my life and always dated people who were bossed up. I still had to boss up on my own. I am not perfect by any means. People who know me know that I do not like to sit still, and I get overwhelmed super easily. I still have a problem being on time, and it's very likely that I'll need to smoke some weed before I walk into any building. I am not afraid of my emotions, but I can definitely be a hothead when I'm upset. If some shit is going down now, I'm feeling it now, and if I need a moment, I need a moment. Trying to talk me into feeling differently, sharing your opinions, or forcing me to process my emotions before I'm ready is only going to make it worse. I don't assume to know how other people are feeling, and I don't want them to try to tap into what I am feeling. I need to be able to express my full range of emotions, and then I can move on. Otherwise, I'll explode. But I'm okay with my imperfections because at the root of it, being the baddest is about knowing who *you* are and making the most out of it.

Acknowledgments

·············· ✦ ··············

TRINA

First and foremost, I would like to thank God for gifting me with a voice that has been able to touch the world. To my beautiful mother, Vernessa Taylor: I could write a book filled with moments that I am able to cherish for the rest of my life. I am forever indebted to your wisdom, your support, your love, and the impression that you have left on our family. To my niece, my daughter that I didn't birth but love limitlessly, Toni "Baby Suga" Chester: You were my ignition in moments when I didn't know I needed it, a reflection of me in every way. Your memory will always live in me. To my brother, Wilbrent "Goonkie" Bain Jr.: I will cherish our bond and memories forever. Thank you for the love that you've always given me, no matter what my choices were. And to my loving best friend and sister, Laura Love: I will always ride with you and for you, no matter the depth. I know the pain that you may feel runs deep as a mother, but I will always be by your side to love you endlessly. You are my calm through the storms, just like our mom, and our sisterly bond is unbreakable. Thank you for always riding for me, even when you have no energy to do so. To my husband, Benjamin, I thank God for you. Thank you for completing me.

This book would not be possible without the support and hard work of Sesali Bowen. You helped me articulate things I'd only thought about, and consider things I hadn't. Thank you for pushing me to be vulnerable and honest while reliving some of the hardest moments. I can't imagine a better person to help bring this vision to life. You started on this project loving Trina, the artist. I'm glad that you now know Katrina, the woman.

To Liberty City (Miami): I am thankful to call you home and for all the support that you've shown me. Ted Lucas, we have had many trials and tribulations throughout my career under Slip-N-Slide Records, but I am thankful to be able to call you my family. Thank you for believing in me! Josh "Redd" Burke, thank you for taking me under your wing as management and helping me and my career to become legendary. I will not ever be able to repay you for the journey under your guidance and protection, but I am blessed to have been able to call on you at any given time for advice. Corey "C.O." Evans, we have had such a ride since day one, and I appreciate you in more than one way. Thank you for defending my legacy and for being loyal to me even in moments that I may have been difficult to deal with. You are one of the core pieces of the team, and I appreciate you. Karen "KD" Douglas, we have been on this journey for seventeen years, and I trust in your feedback, direction, managerial work, and more importantly, your true friendship. Thank you for holding me down over the years, even when I gave you no room to! Aleesha Carter, thank you for being on point with my image, the brand, and my overall well-being, even during the darkest moments. You have truly been at the forefront on my behalf even when I had no strength to be such, and I am thankful to have you on my team. Thank you to Peas and Krystal Coleman.

To all my ROCKSTARRS worldwide: There would be no Trina without your continued support since I was introduced to the world in 1998. Thank you for always being front and center in everything I do. You guys are my extended family, not fans!

To my friend, my mentor, and someone that I admire for your talent and gift to the world, Missy Elliott: Thank you for believing in my career and my artistry and for always being a phone call away. You have always believed in me, even when I haven't, and I will forever be honored to call you my friend.

And to everyone else that I have been able to work with in the music industry—too many to name—thank you for taking a chance on Katrina "Trina" Taylor.

SESALI BOWEN

First and foremost, I have to thank Trina. Thank you for graciously welcoming me into your city and your home. Thank you for being the first person to ever pull up on me in a Wraith, and for showing me the real Miami. Most importantly, thank you for trusting me to help you tell your story. I know it wasn't easy. Both of us were tested by grief and stress during the process, but we made it to the finish line! Thank you for the years of game, pep talks, and inspiration that you've given me through your music. You were the first person to show me how to be the woman I want to be, not the woman everybody expects me to be. You truly helped raise me and a generation of bad bitches. Your legacy lives in all of us.

To Neil Martinez-Belkin: Thank you for being the plug on this one. I appreciate you for dropping gems. You helped me trust this process and reminded me that at the end of the day, shooters shoot and writers write.

Shout-out to the team at Simon & Schuster and DCL. To Lashanda Anakwah: Thank you for believing in and fighting for this project from the beginning. Wishing you so many blessings and success.

I would like to personally dedicate this book to my god-daughter, Aviana Grant. I think of you when I look up at the sky and it reminds me that there's no limit to what I can accomplish. I hope I keep making you proud in heaven.

About the Authors

KATRINA "TRINA" TAYLOR is a platinum-selling hip-hop artist with more than two decades of success in the industry. She has released six studio albums, four EPs, and a multitude of additional recordings in her musical catalog. Her recognitions and nominations include the American Music Awards, Billboard Music Awards, MTV Video Music Awards, and much more. For her long-standing impact in culture and music, BET Networks honored her with the I Am Hip Hop Award in 2022. She is also the creator and producer of the Rockstarr Music Festival, hosted in her hometown. On May 14, 2022, Mayor Francis Suarez presented Trina with a key to the city of Miami.

SESALI BOWEN is the author of the acclaimed memoir-manifesto *Bad Fat Black Girl: Notes from a Trap Feminist* and the creator and host of *Purse First*, the first podcast exclusively about female and queer rap. She oversaw the entertainment vertical at *NYLON* magazine before branching out to write her first book. Her words have appeared in *The New York Times*, *Cosmopolitan*, *Glamour*, *InStyle*, and more. She has also appeared on Netflix's *Explained* and starred in campaigns for Showtime, VH1, and HBO. Behind the scenes, she provides creative marketing and storytelling services to brands and talent. Sesali was proudly born and raised on the South Side of Chicago and currently lives in New Jersey.